Just One Pot

GREAT FOOD, LESS FUSS

DAIRY COOKBOOK

Executive Editor	Nick Rowe
Managing Editor	Emily Anderson
Editor	Emma Callery
Designer	Graham Meigh
Proof Reader	Aune Butt
Indexer	Christine Bernstein
Photographer	Steve Lee
Food Stylist	Sara Lewis
Props Stylist	Jo Harris
Recipes created by	Pat Alburey
	Kathryn Hawkins
	Lucy Knox
	Sue McMahon
	Kate Moseley
Nutritional consultant	Dr Wendy Doyle
Recipe testers	Carolyn Glazebrook
	Barbara Glimmerveen
	Katy Hackforth
	Jean Johnson
	Claudia Linden
	Sandra Meadowcroft
	Christopher Perry
	Kate Timmins
Production	Zoe Fawcett

Eaglemoss Consumer Publications Ltd
Electra House, Electra Way, Crewe, Cheshire, CW1 6WZ
Telephone 01270 270050 Website www.dairydiary.co.uk

First printed March 2009
© Eaglemoss Consumer Publications Ltd
ISBN-13:978-0-9554232-7-7

123456789

Contents

Just One Pot

The relaxed way to prepare good food; no more juggling with lots of pans and different cooking methods, instead a straightforward one-pot approach is all you need – and with the 120 recipes in _Just One Pot_, this is just what you get.

Depending upon your mood, one pot can mean a slow simmering curry, casserole or a quick-fire stir-fry; from snacks right through to glorious desserts _Just One Pot_ produces simple, fresh, home cooked food. All the recipes are quick and easy to prepare and use ingredients that can be purchased easily in mainstream supermarkets.

One-pot cooking is one of the most ancient cooking methods: prehistoric people would bake stones and put them with the food into a clay pot to cook. Once the technology was available, they would then hang or support a metal pot over the fire. In modern times, one-pot cooking might be written off as the choice of bachelors, campers and students, but, in fact, it can efficiently feed snacks or full meals to everyone from singles to families.

Putting together a one-pot recipe is reassuringly straightforward – and there's so little washing up to do afterwards (just the occasional preparation bowl in addition to the pot)! In the age of the ready meal, a one-pot dish is a quick and simple way of preparing tasty wholesome food with all of the nutrition and flavour but no nasty additives. One-pot dishes can boast complex flavours and a variety of textures and the process is remarkably flexible: from soups to creamy risottos, or the rapid blitz of a stir-fry to the gentle simmering of a stew – and there are some truly impressive one-pot desserts.

This book is divided into eight sections, each covering a different method of one-pot cooking. We start with the frying pan – capable of so much more than a traditional fry-up – and move on to saucepan cooking. Then we meet the wok, the mainstay of Eastern cookery for thousands of years. Next up is the casserole, a word so important it is used for the slow-cooking vessel and the dish it contains. For oven-baked dishes that don't require a lid, there's the baking dish, which is followed by the many ways in which a baking sheet and then a roasting tin, can help you prepare

simple but delicious fare. Finally, we work with the humble bowl, in which food can be marinaded, microwaved, or simply arranged for a speedy dish that can be whipped up out of nowhere.

Each section contains a carefully balanced mixture of fish, meat and vegetable dishes, some snacks and some main meals. So many classic main dishes can be made with one pot, such as roasting meat and allowing the juices to soak into the accompanying vegetables before taking everything out of the pan and simmering the remaining liquid down into flavour-packed gravy.

Finally, in most sections there are the sweet dishes, for there are some wonderful one-pot desserts to be made, too – and it is likely to add to your enjoyment when all you have to do is pop one container into the oven while your guests mop up the delicious juices on their plates. When the time comes, just take the dish straight from oven to table and serve.

Within each of these parts of the book are vegetarian and low-fat options to help you create the right meals for your family, whatever their preferences and needs.

Just One Pot is the book that has been designed to make your life streamlined and simple – and, above all, the recipes are truly delicious.

Salad needn't just mean a dull lettuce leaf, a slice of tomato and a little cucumber. Supermarkets now sell such a wide range of salads, from plain rocket to mixed rocket, spinach and watercress, to all manner of continental leaves, some with herbs or delicate fronds of mizuna, that the kind of salads we remember from childhood are now a thing of the past.

Salad accompaniments

Choose from these salad recipes to accompany your one-pot meals.

Dressed leaves
For a bowl of mixed exotic leaves, toss in a little balsamic vinegar, lime or lemon juice or make up a simple vinaigrette with 4 tablespoons of olive oil, 1 tablespoon of red or white vinegar and flavour with ½–1 teaspoon Dijon mustard, sundried tomato paste or ½ clove of finely chopped garlic, some salt and pepper and just a little honey or brown sugar to taste.

Creamy dressed leaves
Cut the calories of mayonnaise-style dressings by mixing half mayonnaise with half low-fat natural yogurt or, for a really low-calorie dressing, use all low-fat natural yogurt and stir in a little grated horseradish sauce, curry paste or crumbled blue cheese. Whisk together and drizzle over a bowl of fresh mixed leaves.

Refreshing salsa
Give tomatoes and cucumber the salsa treatment by dicing and mixing with some diced avocado and red pepper, toss in a little lime or lemon juice and sprinkle with some chopped basil or coriander. Serve spooned into little gem or cos lettuce leaves.

Fruit and nuts
Pep up a carrot, by grating and mixing with a segmented orange, some canned or defrosted frozen sweetcorn and some sprigs of watercress or toasted walnuts, hazelnuts or sunflower seeds, and a few sultanas or raisins. Toss in a Dijon or wholegrain mustard flavoured vinaigrette dressing.

Bean salad
A can of mixed beans can also make a good high-fibre base to any salad. Drain, rinse in cold water and drain again then mix with some halved cherry tomatoes or larger diced tomatoes, some diced raw or roasted red pepper (or some ready roasted from a jar), a little diced red onion and a few torn radicchio, rocket or lettuce leaves. If you don't have any leaves, add some frozen green beans and sweetcorn that have first been plunged into a pan of boiling water for 1 minute then drained. Add to the salad and toss with a mustard dressing or one with a little added sundried tomato paste.

Cook's information

Dry weight conversions

Recommended grams (g)	Imperial ounces (oz)
15	½
25	1
50	2
75	3
110	4 (¼lb)
150	5
175	6
200	7
225	8 (½lb)
250	9
275	10
300	11
350	12 (¾lb)
375	13
400	14
425	15
450	16 (1lb)
500	1lb 2oz
680	1½lb
750	1lb 10oz
900	2lb

These quantities are not exact, but they have been calculated to give proportionately correct measurements.

Liquid conversions

Metric (ml)	Imperial (fl oz)	US cups
15	½	1 tbsp (level)
30	1	⅛
60	2	¼
90	3	⅜
125	4	½
150	5 (¼ pint)	⅔
175	6	¾
225	8	1
300	10 (½ pint)	1¼
350	12	1½
450	16	2
500	18	2¼
600	20 (1 pint)	2½
900	1½ pints	3¾
1 litre	1¾ pints	1 quart (4 cups)
1.25 litres	2 pints	1¼ quarts
1.5 litres	2½ pints	3 US pints
2 litres	3½ pints	2 quarts

| 568ml = 1 UK pint | (20fl oz) | 16fl oz = 1 US pint |

These quantities are not exact, but they have been calculated to give proportionately correct measurements.

Suitable for vegetarians

If you are cooking for a vegetarian, please ensure that any cheese, yogurt or pesto sauce you use is suitable for vegetarians. It should give this information on the jar or packet

Guideline daily amounts: adults

	Women	Men
Energy (calories)	2,000	2,500
Fat (g)	70	95
Saturated fat (g)	20	30
Carbohydrate (g)	230	300
Total sugars (g)	90	120
Protein (g)	45	55
Dietary fibre (g)	24	24
Salt (g)	6	6

Oven temperatures

°C	°F	Gas mark	Description
110	225	¼	cool
120/130	250	½	cool
140	275	1	very low
150	300	2	very low
160/170	325	3	low to moderate
180	350	4	moderate
190	375	5	moderately hot
200	400	6	hot
220	425	7	hot
230	450	8	hot
240	475	9	very hot

Guide to recommended equivalent settings, not exact conversions. Always refer to your cooker instruction book.

Grilling times: fish

Type of fish	Grilling time
Cod (steak)	5–6 min each side
Dover sole (whole)	4–6 min each side
Dover sole (fillet)	2–3 min each side
Halibut (steak)	5–6 min each side
Herring (whole)	4–5 min each side
Mackerel (whole)	6–7 min each side
Monkfish (steak)	5–6 min each side
Plaice (whole)	4–6 min each side
Plaice (fillet)	2–3 min each side
Salmon (steak)	5–6 min each side
Tuna (steak)	1–2 min each side

Times given for fish weighing approximately 175–225g (6–8oz).

Roasting times: meat

Set oven temperature to 180°C/350°F/Gas 4.

	Cooking time per 450g/1lb	Extra cooking time
Beef		
Rare	20 min	20 min
Medium	25 min	25 min
Well done	30 min	30 min
Lamb		
Medium	25 min	25 min
Well done	30 min	30 min
Pork		
Medium	30 min	30 min
Well done	35 min	35 min

Let the cooked meat rest for 5–15 minutes before carving to allow the juices to be reabsorbed and to make carving easier.

Steaming times: vegetables

Vegetable	Steaming time
Asparagus	5–7 min
Beansprouts	3–4 min
Beetroot (sliced)	5–7 min
Broccoli (florets)	5–7 min
Brussels sprouts	5–7 min
Cabbage (chopped)	4–6 min
Cauliflower (florets)	5–7 min
Carrots (thickly sliced)	5–7 min
Courgettes (sliced)	3–5 min
Green beans	5–7 min
Leeks	5–8 min
Mangetout peas	3–5 min
Peas	3–5 min
Potatoes (cubed)	5–7 min

Times given are for steaming from when water has started to boil.

Roasting times: poultry

	Oven temperature	Cooking time per 450g/1lb	Extra cooking time	Resting time
Chicken	200°C/400°F/Gas 6	20 min	30 min	15 min
Turkey (stuffed weight)				
small (under 6kg/13lb)	200°C/400°F/Gas 6	12 min	20 min	30 min
large	180°C/350°F/Gas 4	16 min	—	30 min
Duck	200°C/400°F/Gas 6 for 45 min then 180°C/350°F/Gas 4	35 min	—	15 min

Frying pan

Cooks have used frying pans for thousands of years – copper versions have been found dating back to ancient Mesopotamia, and they were used in ancient Greek and Roman kitchens. They are popular because they offer such a large surface area.

There is no way that frying pans would have lasted all this time if they were only used for basic fry-ups – although there is a classic All-in-one-brunch among these recipes. Other options include Skate with capers, Curried prawns with pitta and, of course, the classic frying pan dish Spanish paella. Wipe down the pan and use it for dessert, too, with Fragrant roasted peaches, Banoffee bread pudding with chocolate and Totally tropical hot fruit salad on the menu.

Preparation time	**20 minutes**
Cooking time	**1 hour 5 minutes, plus cooling**
Calories per portion	**248 Kcal**
Fat per portion	**10.5g**
of which saturated	**2.4g**
Serves	**6**
Suitable for vegetarians	

Spanish tortilla

A simple, scrumptious taste of Spain.

Potatoes 900g (2lb)
Olive oil 2 tbsp
Spanish onion 1, peeled and finely chopped
Garlic 2 cloves, peeled and finely chopped
Eggs 6 large
Salt and freshly ground black pepper
Chopped parsley 1 tbsp

Peel the potatoes and slice very thinly – the thinner you slice the potatoes, the quicker and more evenly they will cook.

Heat the oil in a large, deep frying pan and add the sliced potatoes, onion and garlic. Cook, turning frequently, over a medium heat for about 20 minutes until the potato begins to tenderise, but does not brown.

Beat together the eggs and plenty of seasoning and pour over the potatoes. Keeping the heat low, cook the mixture until set, scraping the egg as it sets round the edge back into the middle, which takes about 30 minutes.

Slide onto a board and then invert back into the pan and continue to cook for a further 15 minutes until completely cooked through.

Remove from the heat and cool for 30 minutes. Cut into wedges and serve sprinkled with parsley.

COOK'S TIP
This tortilla makes perfect picnic food. Allow to cool completely, cut into wedges and store in a plastic container, interleaved with kitchen paper.

Preparation time	10 minutes
Cooking time	35 minutes
Calories per portion	558 Kcal (2 servings)
Fat per portion	33g (2 servings)
of which saturated	18.1g
Serves	2 as main meal, 4 as accompaniment

Suitable for vegetarians

Lancashire layered potatoes

The classic combination of onion, potatoes and cheese makes a tasty midweek meal.

Butter 25g (1oz)
Sunflower oil 1 tbsp
Potatoes 500g (1lb 2oz), peeled and thinly sliced
Onion 1, peeled and sliced
Lancashire cheese 110g (4oz), grated
Salt and freshly ground black pepper

Heat the butter and oil in a solid-based frying pan until the butter has melted. Starting with a layer of potatoes and finishing with a layer of cheese, layer up the potatoes, onion and cheese, seasoning each layer well.

Cover the pan either with a lid or foil, and cook over a gentle heat for 20–30 minutes, or until the potato and onion are tender when pierced with the point of a fine knife.

Remove the cover and cook under a hot grill to brown the top. Serve the dish straight from the pan.

COOK'S TIP
For a meaty, main meal dish, try adding some chopped ham or bacon to the layers of potato.

13

Preparation time	5 minutes
Cooking time	15 minutes
Calories per portion	593 Kcal
Fat per portion	46g
of which saturated	28.8g
Serves	2

Skate with capers

Capers and vinegar perfectly complement the taste of skate.

Plain flour 2 tbsp
Salt and freshly ground black pepper
Skate wings 2 small or 1 large, halved
Butter 110g (4oz)
White wine vinegar 2 tbsp
Capers 2 tbsp, rinsed well and drained
Chopped parsley
Lemon wedges

Tip the flour onto a plate and season it with salt and pepper. Pat the skate dry and dust both sides with the seasoned flour.

Heat half the butter in a large frying pan and cook the skate for 4–5 minutes on each side. Remove the wings from the pan and keep them warm while making the butter sauce.

Add the remaining butter to the pan and heat until it foams and starts to turn to a rich golden brown colour, then pour the vinegar into the pan and add the capers and parsley. Season the sauce to taste.

Place the cooked skate on plates and spoon the sauce over the top. Sprinkle with parsley and serve with a lemon wedge and a Refreshing salsa salad (see page 7).

COOK'S TIP
If your frying pan isn't large enough to cook both skate wings at the same time, then cook them individually rather than having them overlapping in the pan.

Preparation time	**10 minutes**
Cooking time	**5 minutes**
Calories per portion	**389 Kcal**
Fat per portion	**15g**
of which saturated	**2.1g**
Serves	**4**

Curried prawns with pitta

Succulent and subtly spiced prawns on a bed of peppery leaves.

Pitta breads 4
Olive oil 3 tbsp
Garlic 12 large cloves, peeled and crushed
Paprika 1 tsp
Ground cumin 1 tsp
Ground ginger ½ tsp
Frozen peeled tiger prawns 350g (12oz), thawed
Bunch of coriander chopped
Salt and freshly ground black pepper
Pine nuts 25g (1oz)
Rocket leaves 50g packet
Watercress 75g packet
Onion 1, peeled and thinly sliced
Natural yogurt 4 tbsp
Lemon 1, quartered

Preheat the oven to 160°C/325°C/ Gas 3 and place the pitta breads in it to warm.

Heat the oil in a frying pan and add the garlic and spices. Stir over a low heat for 1 minute.

Increase the heat to high and add the prawns. Stir-fry for 2 minutes or until they turn pink. Add the coriander and cook for another 30 seconds. Season, then mix with the pine nuts.

Remove the pitta breads from the oven, tear them in half and place one on each plate. Divide the rocket, watercress and onion slices between the plates. Spoon the prawns and their juices on to the leaves.

Serve with a generous dollop of yogurt and a squeeze of lemon juice over the prawns.

COOK'S TIP
Not a fan of prawns? Then dice 4 small boneless chicken breasts and fry for 8–10 minutes in the oil and spices until golden brown and cooked through.

Preparation time	10 minutes
Cooking time	10 minutes
Calories per portion	239 Kcal
Fat per portion	15g
of which saturated	4.9g
Serves	4

Pan-fried bacon & scallops with salad

A traditional combination of textures and flavours – and quick to cook.

Smoked bacon lardons 200g (7oz)
Scallops about 16 weighing 400g (14oz), trimmed
Olive oil 1 tbsp, plus extra for serving (optional)
Limes 3, juice of 1 and the rest cut into wedges to serve
Freshly ground black pepper
Mixed herb salad 75g packet

COOK'S TIP
To be sure the scallops are ready – they don't take long – cut one in half and check it is white all the way through.

Heat a large frying pan. Add the lardons and cook over a high heat for 5–6 minutes, stirring. Put the scallops in a large bowl and add the olive oil, lime juice and freshly ground black pepper. Stir together gently.

Remove the scallops and discard any leftover oil mix. Push the bacon to the edge of the pan. Turn the heat down to medium and carefully arrange the scallops in the middle, making sure they don't overlap. Cook for 4–6 minutes, turning once or until just tender. The exact cooking time will depend on the thickness and size of the scallops.

Arrange the salad on four plates, drizzle with a little extra oil (if wished) and serve the scallops and bacon on the salad leaves. Serve hot with lime wedges.

Preparation time	**15 minutes**
Cooking time	**35–40 minutes**
Calories per portion	**477 Kcal**
Fat per portion	**9g**
of which saturated	**1.5g**
Serves	**4–6**

Spanish paella

Authentic Spanish rice with seafood and chicken.

Olive oil 2 tbsp
Red onion 1, peeled and chopped
Garlic 2 cloves, peeled and crushed
Red pepper 1, deseeded and chopped
Skinless, boneless chicken breasts 2, cubed
Saffron 3–4 strands
Spanish paella rice 250g (9oz)
Fish or vegetable stock 1 litre (1¾ pints)
Frozen peas 110g (4oz)
Raw large prawns 225g (8oz)
Scallops 225g (8oz) trimmed
Salt and freshly ground black pepper
Chopped parsley 2 tbsp
Lemons 4, cut into wedges

Heat the oil in a paella pan or large frying pan. Add the onion, garlic and red pepper and cook for 5 minutes or until softened. Add the chicken breasts and cook for 5 minutes, stirring, or until the chicken is golden.

Add the saffron and rice and stir-fry for 2 minutes. Add the stock and cook for 20–25 minutes, until the rice is just tender.

Fold in the peas, prawns and scallops and continue cooking for 3–5 minutes or until the shellfish are cooked through. Season to taste.

Serve scattered with fresh herbs and plenty of fresh lemon wedges

COOK'S TIP
Paella rice is available in the rice section of supermarkets. If you can't find paella rice, then substitute with risotto rice.

Preparation time	10 minutes
Cooking time	30 minutes
Calories per portion	355 Kcal
Fat per portion	17.6g
of which saturated	6g
Serves	4

Suitable for freezing

Hungarian chicken

A colourful, creamy chicken dish with piquant paprika.

Olive oil 2–3 tbsp
Skinless chicken breasts 500g (1lb 2oz), cut into strips
Onion 1 large, halved and sliced
Green pepper 1, deseeded and thinly sliced
Red pepper 1, deseeded and thinly sliced
Plain flour 2 tbsp
Sweet paprika 2 tsp
Chicken stock 225ml (8fl oz)
Sun-dried tomato paste 2–3 tbsp
Salt and freshly ground black pepper
Soured cream 150ml (5fl oz)
Pickled gherkins 4, cut into thin strips

Heat the oil in a large lidded frying pan. Add the chicken and cook over a moderate-high heat until lightly browned, then remove from the pan.

Add the onion and peppers to the oil remaining in the pan and cook gently until softened.

Return the chicken to the pan, stir in the flour and paprika, add the stock and tomato paste and bring to the boil, stirring. Reduce the heat, cover and simmer gently for 15–20 minutes until the chicken is tender.

Season the chicken with salt and freshly ground black pepper and serve with ready cooked rice heated in a microwave, topped with soured cream sprinkled with gherkins.

COOK'S TIP
Cut costs by buying two packs of mini chicken breast fillets when premium skinless breasts are not on offer. Alternatively, substitute the same weight of turkey breast.

Preparation time	**5 minutes**
Cooking time	**40 minutes**
Calories per portion	**586 Kcal**
Fat per portion	**35g**
of which saturated	**20.8g**
Serves	**4**
Suitable for freezing	

Apricot chicken

With a sweet, slightly tangy sauce the chicken is tender and full of flavour.

Butter 50g (2oz)
New potatoes 500g (1lb 2oz), scrubbed and quartered
Chicken breasts 4, skin left on
Apricots in juice 411g can
Crème fraîche 200ml carton
Frozen peas 110g (4oz)
Salt and freshly ground black pepper

Melt half the butter in a deep frying pan. Add the potatoes and cook them over a medium heat for 10–15 minutes, turning occasionally, until they are a light golden colour and are just tender. Remove the potatoes from the pan.

Add the remaining butter to the pan and heat it to melt it. Add the chicken breasts, skin side down, and cook for 4–5 minutes. Then turn over and cook for a further 4–5 minutes over a medium heat, until the chicken is cooked through.

Return the potatoes to the pan and heat through, then pour in the juice from the apricots. Chop the apricots and add them to the pan too. Bring to a simmer, and simmer for 4–5 minutes, until the juice goes syrupy.

Add the crème fraîche to the pan, bring the mixture to a simmer and cook for 4–5 minutes until the sauce starts to thicken. Add the peas to the pan and cook for a further 2–3 minutes, or until the peas are just cooked and the sauce is a good consistency and not too runny. Season to taste and serve immediately.

COOK'S TIP
If you need to speed up the cooking time a little, skin the chicken breasts and cut them into chunks and then stir-fry for 5–6 minutes, or until the chicken is cooked.

Preparation time	**10 minutes**
Cooking time	**16 minutes**
Calories per portion	**229 Kcal**
Fat per portion	**6g**
of which saturated	**1.6g**
Serves	**4**
Suitable for freezing	

Pork with blackberries & apple

Fat juicy blackberries with soft apple complement the texture of the pork.

Vegetable oil 1 tbsp
Lean pork fillet 450g (1lb), trimmed and thinly sliced
Unsweetened apple juice 150ml (¼ pint)
Chicken stock 150ml (¼ pint)
Clear honey 1 tbsp
Chopped sage 1 tbsp
Salt and freshly ground black pepper
Granny Smith apples 2, cored and sliced
Blackberries 150g (5oz)
Cornflour 2 tsp

Heat the oil in a non-stick medium-sized frying pan. Add the sliced pork and cook for about 3 minutes on each side until browned all over and the juices run. Using a draining spoon, transfer the pork to a plate lined with kitchen paper and set aside.

Pour the apple juice and stock into the frying pan and add the honey, sage and seasoning. Bring to the boil, stirring, and reduce to a simmer, then return the pork to the pan and add the apples. Cover the pan and cook gently for 5 minutes.

Add the blackberries, cover and cook gently for a further 5 minutes. Blend the cornflour with 4 teaspoons cold water to make a paste and stir into the mixture. Raise the heat slightly and cook for about a minute, stirring, until lightly thickened. Serve with crusty bread and coleslaw.

COOK'S TIP
If fresh blackberries are unavailable, use frozen or even canned blackberries in natural juice instead.

Preparation time	**15 minutes**
Cooking time	**20 minutes**
Calories per portion	**543 Kcal**
Fat per portion	**43g**
of which saturated	**12.4g**
Serves	**2**

All-in-one-brunch

Hearty and delicious, the perfect weekend breakfast.

Thick pork sausages 3
Vegetable oil 1 tbsp
Smoked back bacon 2 rashers,
trimmed and halved
Large flat mushroom 1, peeled,
wiped and thickly sliced
Large vine tomato 1, thickly sliced
Eggs 3 large, beaten
**Salt and freshly ground black
pepper**

COOK'S TIP
Use a good non-stick frying pan so that
the egg doesn't stick to the bottom of
it. Add a little wholegrain mustard to the
eggs when beating.

Slice the sausages through the middle lengthways. Heat the oil in a medium-sized frying pan and gently fry the sausages, cut side down, for 5 minutes until lightly browned.

Turn the sausages over, add the bacon and cook for a further 5 minutes, turning the bacon over after 2 minutes. Using cooking tongs or two forks, transfer to a heat-proof plate and set aside.

Add the mushroom and tomato to the same pan and cook in the meat juices, turning occasionally, for about 5 minutes until cooked through and tender.

Return the meat to the pan and arrange the contents evenly over the bottom. Then pour the beaten eggs into the pan, season well and cook gently for 3–4 minutes until the egg just sets.

Serve immediately, straight from the pan with freshly toasted bread.

23

Preparation time	20 minutes
Cooking time	30–40 minutes
Calories per portion	856 Kcal
Fat per portion	50g
of which saturated	14.3g
Serves	2
Suitable for freezing	

Cumberland sausage with red cabbage

Vibrant softened red cabbage topped with traditional English sausage.

Cumberland sausage rings 2x 225g (8oz) rings
Olive oil 1 tbsp
Small potatoes 350–400g (12 –14oz), cut into slices about 5mm (¼in) thick
Small onions 225–250g (8–9oz), peeled and halved lengthways
Red cabbage 400g (14oz) piece, trimmed, woody centre removed and shredded
Runner beans 150g (5oz), trimmed and cut diagonally into long thin strips
Chicken stock 300ml (½ pint)
Balsamic vinegar

Wipe the sausage rings dry with kitchen paper and secure the end of the rings with a cocktail stick to stop them unravelling during cooking. Heat the oil in a very large, lidded frying pan – preferably non-stick.

Add the sausage rings to the pan and cook for 2–3 minutes on each side until browned, then remove from the pan onto a plate and set aside.

Add the sliced potatoes, onions and cabbage to the pan and cook for 4–5 minutes, until the potatoes are lightly browned. Then add the runner beans.

Pour the stock over the vegetables and place the Cumberland rings on top. Cover the pan with a lid and cook gently for 30–40 minutes, or until the vegetables are tender and the sausage rings are cooked through. To serve, toss the cabbage in a little balsamic vinegar and spoon onto warmed plates. Top with the sausage rings with the cocktail sticks removed.

COOK'S TIP
All the vegetables can be washed and prepared ahead of cooking time and stored in a covered container in the refrigerator.

Preparation time	10 minutes
Cooking time	15 minutes
Calories per portion	394 Kcal
Fat per portion	23g
of which saturated	7.5g
Serves	4

Liver & bacon

A classic combination of succulent meats.

Olive oil 2 tbsp
Onions 2 large, peeled, halved and sliced
Smoked back bacon 8 rashers, rind removed and cut into strips
Lamb's liver 450g (1lb), cleaned and sliced
Cayenne pepper a pinch
Plain flour 1 tbsp
Fresh gravy 300g pot
Worcestershire sauce 1 tbsp
Irish soda farls 2, halved and toasted
Baby spinach 2 x 180g packs

Heat the oil in a large, heavy-based non-stick frying pan. Cook the onions over a medium heat, stirring occasionally, for at least 10 minutes, until they are softened and golden.

Add the bacon to the pan and cook for about 5 minutes. Meanwhile, toss the slices of liver in the cayenne pepper and flour.

Add the liver to the pan and cook over a high heat until the liver is just cooked, stirring. Add the pot of gravy and Worcestershire sauce and bring to the boil. Reduce the heat and simmer for 2–5 minutes until thickened, to taste.

Toast the farls and cook the spinach in the microwave in its bag according to the packet's instructions. To serve, divide the spinach between warmed plates, top with the farls and then with the liver and bacon.

COOK'S TIP
If you can't find farls in your supermarket, substitute breakfast muffins or 4 slices of toasted granary bread instead.

Preparation time	**15 minutes**
Cooking time	**1½–1¾ hours**
Calories per portion	**721 Kcal**
Fat per portion	**41.9g**
of which saturated	**19.8g**
Serves	**4**

Suitable for freezing without the dumplings

Slow-cooked lamb with dumplings

Traditional comfort food at its best.

For the stew:
Butter 50g (2oz)
Vegetable oil 1 tbsp
Lamb 350g (12oz) leg, diced
Onion 1, peeled and cut into thin wedges
Red-skinned potatoes 2, peeled and cut into chunks
Carrots 2, peeled and cut into chunks
Parsnip 2, peeled and cut into chunks
Swede ½, peeled and cut into chunks
Plain flour 2 tbsp
Lamb stock cube 1
Worcestershire sauce a dash
Salt and freshly ground black pepper

For the dumplings
Self-raising flour 150g (5oz)
Shredded vegetable or beef suet 75g (3oz)
Chopped rosemary 2 tbsp

COOK'S TIP
You may need to top up the frying pan with a little extra stock. Check the pan after an hour to see if this is the case.

Heat half the butter and the oil in a large, lidded frying pan and add the lamb. Cook the meat for 5–8 minutes, turning the meat occasionally until it has browned on all surfaces, then remove it from the pan.

Add the remaining butter to the pan and heat until it's bubbling, then add the onion and vegetables and cook for 4–5 minutes. Stir the flour into the pan and cook the vegetables for 1–2 minutes, then gradually stir in 600ml (1 pint) water, bringing the pan's contents to the boil between each addition to make a smooth gravy.

Crumble in the stock cube and stir until dissolved. Return the meat to the pan. Bring the stew to a gentle simmer, cover and simmer gently for 1 hour. Stir in the Worcestershire sauce and seasoning to taste.

To make the dumplings, sift the flour into a bowl. Stir in the suet, rosemary and seasoning and add enough water to make a soft dough. Divide the dough into 12, shape into balls and place on top of the stew. Cover the pan and simmer for about 15 minutes, until the dumplings have risen. Serve immediately.

Preparation time	**10 minutes**	
Cooking time	**10 minutes**	
Calories per portion	**869 Kcal**	
Fat per portion	**48g**	
of which saturated	**26g**	
Serves	**2**	

Quick beef & mushroom stroganoff

A rich and creamy dish and a great way to split one steak between two.

Butter 15g (½oz)
Olive oil 2 tsp
Leek 1, trimmed and finely sliced
Garlic 1 clove, peeled and sliced
Fresh penne or similar pasta 150g (5oz)
Mangetout 50g (2oz)
Trimmed rump steak 225g (8oz), cut into finger-width strips
Chestnut mushrooms 110g (4oz), wiped and sliced
Dry white wine 100ml (3½ fl oz)
Crème fraîche 150ml pot (or soured cream 142ml pot)
Wholegrain mustard 2 tsp
English mustard 1 tsp
Salt and freshly ground black pepper
Chopped tarragon 2 tbsp (optional)

COOK'S TIP
Chestnut mushrooms are best to use as they are firm, keep their shape and don't give off liquid, which would colour the sauce.

Heat the butter and oil in a large frying pan. Add the leek and garlic and cook for 2 minutes. Use a slotted spoon to transfer the softened leek to a plate.

Meanwhile, put the pasta in a mixing bowl, add the mangetout and pour over enough boiling water to cover. Leave to stand as instructed on the packet (about 4 minutes). Add the beef and then the mushrooms to the hot frying pan and cook for 2–3 minutes, until browned. Pour in the wine and simmer for a couple of minutes.

Stir in the crème fraîche (or soured cream) and the two mustards and bring just to the boil. Add the leeks and drained pasta and mangetout. Heat through and check the pasta is cooked, season and sprinkle with tarragon, if using, for serving. Serve hot, with Dressed leaf salad (page 7).

Preparation time	**20 minutes**
Cooking time	**15–20 minutes**
Calories per portion	**98 Kcal**
Fat per portion	**2g**
of which saturated	**0.2g**
Serves	**6**

Suitable for vegetarians
Suitable for freezing

Fragrant poached peaches

A scrumptious and velvety dessert.

Firm but ripe peaches 6 large
Cinnamon stick 5cm (2in) piece, halved
Rosé wine 500ml (18fl oz)
Caster sugar 25g (1oz)
Orange 1 large, very finely pared rind and strained juice
Half fat crème fraîche or quark or low fat natural yogurt
Sliced pistachio nuts

COOK'S TIP
If serving the peaches cold, they will last well if they are prepared and cooked the day before you plan on eating them.

Cut the peaches in half and carefully remove the stones. Place the peach halves in a single layer in a lidded frying pan. Add the cinnamon stick pieces, wine, sugar, orange rind and juice.

Place the pan over a moderate heat and bring the wine up to the boil. Reduce the heat, cover with the lid and gently cook the peaches for 5–10 minutes (depending on their size), until they are only just softened when tested with the tip of a knife.

When the peaches are cooked, remove the pan from the heat. Using a large slotted spoon, remove the peaches from the wine and transfer them into a large heat-proof serving dish.

Return the frying pan to the heat, bring the wine back up to the boil and then boil gently until the wine is reduced by about two-thirds or until slightly syrupy.

Pour the wine over the peaches and allow them to cool. When cold, cover and refrigerate until well chilled. Serve with crème fraîche, quark or yogurt and sprinkled with pistachio nuts. If preferred, the peaches may also be served hot.

Preparation time	**10 minutes**
Cooking time	**10 minutes**
Calories per portion	**289 Kcal**
Fat per portion	**17g**
of which saturated	**8.2g**
Serves	**4**

Suitable for vegetarians

Fruity baked custard

This fluffy pudding is perfect autumnal comfort food.

Cox's apples 2 large, peeled, cored and thinly sliced
Plums 225g (8oz), halved, stoned and cut into wedges
Butter 15g (½oz)
Sugar 40g (1½oz)
Ground cloves ½ tsp
Ground cinnamon ½ tsp
Eggs 4
Soured cream 142ml tub

Put the apples, plums, butter and half of the sugar in a large frying pan. Cook over a low heat until the fruit is softened, stirring continuously. Add the cloves and cinnamon. Stir well and remove from the heat.

Separate the eggs, so the whites are in a mixing bowl and the yolks in a small container. Whisk the egg whites until stiff. Fold the eggs very gently into the fruit. Wipe out the bowl and then beat the egg yolks with the soured cream and fold gently into the fruit.

Cook over a low heat until the mixture has set. Then sprinkle with the remaining sugar and brown under a hot grill. Serve immediately, while hot, with soured cream or natural yogurt.

COOK'S TIP
If your frying pan has a plastic handle, take care it doesn't melt when browning the custard under the grill.

Preparation time	**15 minutes**
Cooking time	**5 minutes**
Calories per portion	**320 Kcal**
Fat per portion	**19g**
of which saturated	**3.5g**
Serves	**4**

Suitable for vegetarians

Totally tropical hot fruit salad

A comforting combination of sweet juicy fruit cooked in creamy coconut.

Small papaya 1
Medium pineapple ½
Small mango 1
Unsalted butter 50g (2oz)
Demerara sugar 50g (2oz)
Canned coconut milk 200ml (7fl oz)
Dark rum 2 tbsp (optional)
Vanilla extract 1 tsp
Lime 1 small, grated zest and 2 tbsp juice

Halve the papaya lengthways and scoop out the seeds, then peel off the skin and cut into thin wedges. Cut the pineapple in half and slice off the skin and remove all the 'eyes' from the flesh. Slice out the core and cut the flesh into chunks. Set aside.

For the mango, peel the skin using a vegetable peeler. Slice down either side of the smooth flat central stone, and cut the flesh into thin wedges.

Melt the butter in a large frying pan with the sugar until bubbling and stir in the coconut milk. Bring to simmering point then add the fruit. Cook, stirring occasionally, for 5 minutes until the fruit is hot. Stir in the rum, if using, along with the vanilla extract.

Spoon into warmed serving bowls and serve with the lime zest and juice sprinkled on top.

COOK'S TIP
To save time, use pre-cut tropical fruit salad mix or a frozen fruit mix.

Preparation time	**10 minutes**
Cooking time	**10 minutes**
Calories per pancake	**75 Kcal**
Fat per pancake	**3g**
of which saturated	**1.6g**
Makes	**20 pancakes**
Suitable for vegetarians	

Scotch pancakes

Perfect for breakfast or supper, spread with strawberry jam.

Self-raising flour 225g (8oz)
Salt a pinch
Butter 50g (2oz)
Golden caster sugar 25g (1oz)
Egg 1, beaten
Milk 225ml (8fl oz)
Sunflower oil 1 tbsp
Butter, honey or jam

COOK'S TIP
Don't have the heat too high when cooking the pancakes or they will scorch before they are cooked through.

Sift the flour and salt into a bowl. Rub in the butter and stir in the sugar. Make a well in the centre and add the beaten egg. Whisk in the milk gradually working in the flour until the batter has a consistency of softly whipped cream.

Wipe a non-stick frying pan with kitchen paper dipped in a little sunflower oil. Heat the pan until hot. Turn down the heat.

Cook the pancakes in batches. Drop tablespoons of the mix onto the pan. Fry for 1–2 minutes on each side or until the surface puffs and bubbles slightly. Eat warm with butter and jam or honey.

31

Preparation time	10 minutes
Cooking time	6 minutes
Calories per portion	476 Kcal
Fat per portion	21g
of which saturated	11.2g
Serves	4

Suitable for vegetarians

Banoffee bread pudding with chocolate

A decadent, fluffy dessert served with banana and cream – bliss.

White bread 4 thick slices, crusts removed
Golden syrup 110g (4oz)
Butter 50g (2oz)
Light brown sugar 50g (2oz)
Banana 1 large, peeled and sliced
Plain chocolate chips 50g (2oz)
Double cream 4 tbsp

Cut the bread into 16 equal triangles and set aside. Put the syrup, butter and sugar in a large frying pan and heat gently, stirring, until melted.

Bring slowly to the boil, then carefully place the bread triangles into the bubbling syrup. Press them down and then turn them over. Reduce the heat and cook gently for 6 minutes, turning after 3 minutes, until richly golden.

Turn off the heat – the heat will stay in the dish for a long while. Sprinkle with the sliced banana and chocolate chips and serve immediately, straight from the pan, drizzled with the cream.

COOK'S TIP
When cooking the bread in the toffee sauce, keep the heat low and a careful eye on the sauce so the sugar doesn't 'catch' and burn.

Saucepan

From soups to pasta to stewed fruit, the saucepan is as versatile as any other pot in the kitchen.

Soups such as Carrot & tomato or Vegetable & pasta are classic one-pot dishes, while the Parsnip & apple soup is an unusual variation. Scrambled eggs with smoked salmon is a luxurious take on a kitchen staple, and you can try more complicated recipes, too, such as Stuffed chicken with bacon. Saucepans are just perfect for pasta dishes, such as Creamy herby pasta and Garlic mushroom tagliatelle. Puddings include the wonderfully decadent Cider-soaked fruit or the spicy Gingered gooseberry fool.

Preparation time	**15 minutes**
Cooking time	**30 minutes**
Calories per portion	**130 Kcal**
Fat per portion	**5g**
of which saturated	**0.6g**
Serves	**6**

Suitable for vegetarians

Suitable for freezing

Carrot & tomato soup

The ideal storecupboard soup, with a subtle spicy flavour.

Olive oil 2 tbsp
Onions 2 large, peeled and roughly chopped
Carrots 680g (1½lb), peeled and sliced
Medium curry powder 1½–2 tbsp
Chopped tomatoes 1 x 400g can
Vegetable stock or water 1.5 litres (2½ pints)
Fresh coriander finely chopped, to garnish, optional

Heat the olive oil in a large saucepan, add the onions and cook gently for 10–15 minutes until softened, taking care not to let them brown.

Add the carrots, curry powder, tomatoes and stock or water. Bring to the boil, then reduce the heat, partially cover the pan with a lid and cook the vegetables for 25–30 minutes, or until the carrots are softened.

Remove the pan from the heat and allow the soup to cool a little. Purée it, in batches, in a food processor or blender. If necessary, adjust the consistency of the soup with a little additional vegetable stock or water.

Return the puréed soup to the pan and reheat gently. Serve garnished with a sprinkling of chopped coriander.

COOK'S TIP
Sweet potato soup could also be made in the same way, substituting the sweet potato for the same weight of carrots.

Preparation time	**15 minutes**
Cooking time	**30 minutes**
Calories per portion	**195 Kcal**
Fat per portion	**8.5g**
of which saturated	**2g**
Serves	**4**

Suitable for vegetarians if using a Parmesan substitute

Vegetable & pasta soup

An attractive soup full of texture and colour.

Oil 2 tbsp
Onion 1, peeled and chopped
Garlic 1 fat clove, peeled and chopped
Carrot 1, peeled and diced
Celery 2 sticks, chopped
Potato 1, peeled and diced
Courgette 1 medium to large, trimmed and diced
Green beans 100g (3½oz), trimmed and cut into short lengths
Vegetable stock 1.25 litres (2 pints)
Mini pasta (conchigliette or similar) 50g (2oz)
Frozen peas 50g (2oz)
Tomatoes 2, deseeded and diced
Salt and freshly ground black pepper
Chopped parsley a good handful
Grated Parmesan cheese 2 tsp per person

Heat the oil in a large, deep, lidded saucepan. Add the onion, garlic, carrot and celery and fry gently for 5 minutes. Add the potato, courgette and beans and cook for another 5 minutes with the lid on the saucepan.

Pour in 1 litre (1¾ pints) of the stock. Bring to the boil for 5 minutes and then add the pasta, part cover and cook for 10 minutes, adding more stock if you like. Tip in the peas and then, after another couple of minutes, add the tomato and leave the soup to simmer for 1–2 minutes more, until the tomato is warmed through.

Season well. Spoon into bowls and sprinkle with lots of parsley and freshly grated Parmesan cheese.

COOK'S TIP
If you have a jar of pesto in the fridge, you might like to stir half a teaspoon into each portion just before sprinkling with the Parmesan cheese.

Preparation time	10 minutes
Cooking time	40 minutes
Calories per portion	172 Kcal
Fat per portion	10g
of which saturated	5.2g
Serves	6

Suitable for freezing

Suitable for vegetarians

Parsnip & apple soup

Sweet parsnip combines perfectly with a hint of tart cooking apple.

Butter 50g (2oz)
Dessert apple 1, cored, peeled and sliced
Parsnips 680g (1½lb), peeled and sliced
Bramley cooking apple 1, cored, peeled and sliced
Vegetable stock 1.25 litres (2 pints)
Sage leaves 4, plus extra to garnish
Whole cloves 2
Single cream 150ml (¼ pint)
Salt and freshly ground black pepper

Melt half the butter in a large saucepan and add the dessert apple slices. Sauté until lightly browned, remove and set aside. Melt the remaining butter and add the parsnips and cooking apple. Cover and cook gently for 10 minutes, stirring occasionally.

Pour the stock into the saucepan and add the sage and cloves. Bring to the boil, cover and then simmer for 30 minutes, until the parsnip is softened.

Remove the sage leaves and cloves, then purée in a blender or food processor. Return to the saucepan and reheat gently with the cream. Season to taste. Serve hot, garnished with the sage leaves and apple slices and serve with granary bread.

COOK'S TIP
If you prefer, use ½ tsp of dried sage when cooking the parsnips. For a lower fat version, simply omit the cream – the soup still tastes really good.

Preparation time	25 minutes
Cooking time	30 minutes
Calories per portion	118 Kcal
Fat per portion	8.5g
of which saturated	4.2g
Serves	4

Suitable for vegetarians
Suitable for freezing

Mushroom soup

Gorgeous creamy soup with a meaty mushroom flavour.

Butter 25g (1oz)
Onion 1 large, peeled and finely chopped
Dried porcini mushrooms 15g (½oz), soaked in 225ml (8fl oz) boiling water
Large, flat, brown-skinned mushrooms 400g (14oz), wiped and roughly chopped
Vegetable stock 600ml (1 pint)
Milk 500ml (18fl oz)
Lemon 1, juice only
Single cream
Toasted pine nuts
Snipped chives

Melt the butter in a saucepan, add the onion and cook over a moderate heat until softened but not browned.

Strain the liquid from the porcini and add the drained porcini with the fresh mushrooms to the saucepan. Stir in the stock and milk and bring just to the boil. Reduce the heat, cover and cook for 30 minutes.

Allow the soup to cool slightly and purée in a blender or food processor. Season well, and add lemon juice to taste. Serve with a swirl of cream and toasted pine nuts and chives.

COOK'S TIP
Dried porcini add a rich depth to this soup; they also taste good made into risotto for a store cupboard supper topped with a little crispy bacon or grated cheese.

Preparation time	**10 minutes**
Cooking time	**30 minutes**
Calories per portion	**89 Kcal**
Fat per portion	**7g**
of which saturated	**3.5g**
Serves	**4**

Mediterranean tomato soup

For a taste of sunshine, the soup is both easy to make and delicious.

Olive oil 2 tsp
Unsalted butter 25g (1oz)
Onions 2 small, peeled and chopped
Carrots 2, peeled and finely diced
Celery 2 sticks, diced
Basil ½ bunch, chopped
Tarragon ½ bunch, chopped
Bay leaf 1
Garlic 1 large clove, peeled and crushed
Smoked back bacon 3 rashers, de-rinded and chopped
Plum tomatoes 450g (1lb) skinned
Chicken stock 300–400ml (10–14fl oz)
Tomato purée (optional)
Salt and freshly ground black pepper
Parmesan shavings

COOK'S TIP
Alternatively, top each bowl of soup with a slice of toasted French bread rubbed with a cut clove of garlic and sprinkled with a little crumbled Dolcelatte cheese.

Heat the oil and butter in a large saucepan. Add the onions, carrots and celery and cook gently for 2–3 minutes. Add the herbs (reserving some of the basil for serving) and garlic and cook for 2–3 minutes. Add the bacon and cook for 5 minutes until the vegetables are slightly soft.

Cut each tomato into 8 segments, add to the pan and cook gently for about 5 minutes, stirring occasionally.

Once the tomatoes have broken down, add the stock, a ladle at a time. Use purée for a deeper colour. Cook for 10 minutes before seasoning.

To serve, ladle into warmed bowls and then sprinkle with Parmesan shavings and the reserved chopped basil over the top.

Preparation time	**10 minutes, plus possible soaking time**
Cooking time	**20 minutes**
Calories per portion	**308 Kcal**
Fat per portion	**5g**
of which saturated	**1.8g**
Serves	**6**
Suitable for freezing	

Pea & bacon soup

Wholesome and traditional, this is a real winter-warmer.

Split dried peas 450g (1lb)
Streaky bacon 3 rashers, de-rinded and chopped
Onion 1, peeled and roughly chopped
Carrot 1, peeled and diced
Celery 1 stick, chopped
Chicken or ham stock 2.5 litres (4 pints)
Salt and freshly ground black pepper
Double cream 6 tbsp (optional)
Grilled bacon chopped

If the dried peas need soaking, do this first, following the manufacturer's instructions.

Put the bacon, onion, carrot and celery in a large saucepan and cook for 5–10 minutes, until they are beginning to soften.

Add the soaked peas and the stock and bring to the boil. Boil rapidly, uncovered for 10 minutes, then cover and simmer for around an hour, until the peas are tender.

Allow to cool slightly, then purée the soup in a blender or food processor, until smooth.

Return the soup to the pan. Season to taste, and reheat gently. Serve hot, with a swirl of cream, if using, and garnished with the chopped bacon.

COOK'S TIP
For a vegetarian version, omit the bacon and replace the meat stock with vegetable stock.

Preparation time	**10 minutes**
Cooking time	**15 minutes**
Calories per portion	**319 Kcal**
Fat per portion	**10g**
of which saturated	**2.6g**
Serves	**4**

Suitable for vegetarians

Creamy herby pasta

Light and colourful with seasonal vegetables – just add what is freshest.

Pasta, such as penne, twists or bows 225g (8oz)
Asparagus spears 8, woody ends trimmed and the spears cut into 5cm (2in) lengths
Peas, fresh or frozen 110g (4oz)
Spinach 110g (4oz), washed and drained and torn into strips
Half fat crème fraîche 5 tbsp
Capers 1 tbsp, rinsed and chopped if large
Lemon juice 1 tsp
Salt and freshly ground black pepper
Mint leaves a handful, shredded
Basil leaves a handful, shredded
Toasted pine nuts 3 tbsp

COOK'S TIP
To toast pine nuts, heat the saucepan, add the pine nuts and stir over a medium heat until evenly coloured. Don't walk away from them as they toast surprisingly quickly.

Add the pasta to a large saucepan of boiling water. Stir well and when it comes back to the boil, cook for 5 minutes. Add the asparagus, return to the boil and add the peas, then simmer another 3–4 minutes until the pasta is just getting tender.

Drain the pasta well. Put the spinach in the pasta pan and tip the pasta and vegetables on top. Stir gently so that the spinach starts to wilt.

Stir in the crème fraîche, capers and lemon juice and add seasoning to taste, keeping the pan over a low heat for a couple of minutes to heat everything through. Add the shredded mint and most of the shredded basil leaves.

Spoon the pasta mixture into hot serving dishes and sprinkle with pine nuts and the rest of the basil leaves. Serve immediately while hot.

43

Preparation time **20 minutes**
Cooking time **25 minutes**
Calories per portion **733 Kcal**
Fat per portion **50g**
of which saturated **23.9g**
Serves **4**
Suitable for vegetarians if using a Parmesan substitute

Garlic mushroom tagliatelle

Flavoursome Italian comfort food.

Olive oil 3 tbsp
Salt and freshly ground black pepper
Dried tagliatelle 300–400g (11–14oz)
Red onion 1 large, peeled and chopped
Garlic 2 cloves, peeled and crushed
Portabella mushrooms 250g punnet, wiped and sliced

Oyster mushrooms 125g punnet, wiped and thickly sliced
Baby mushrooms 150g punnet, wiped and halved
Double cream 300ml pot
Chopped parsley 2 tbsp
Parmesan cheese shavings

Bring a large saucepan of water with 1 tablespoon of the olive oil and a little salt to the boil. Add the pasta and cook according to the packet's instructions – usually 10–12 minutes. Drain.

Rinse and dry the pan. Add the remaining oil. Cook the onion over a medium heat in the saucepan with the garlic, until softened and golden.

Add the mushrooms and cook for about 5 minutes, stirring, or until the mushrooms have softened. Add the cream and bring to the boil. Reduce the heat and simmer for 2–5 minutes or until slightly thickened.

Add the pasta and, always stirring, cook until it is heated through. Divide the pasta between four warmed pasta plates and serve with a scattering of fresh parsley, freshly ground black pepper and grated Parmesan.

COOK'S TIP
To make life easier, prepare the onion, garlic, mushrooms and parsley while the pasta is cooking.

Preparation time	**4 minutes**
Cooking time	**3 minutes**
Calories per portion	**766 Kcal**
Fat per portion	**55g**
of which saturated	**25.2g**
Serves	**2**

Scrambled eggs with smoked salmon

A European twist on this classic breakfast dish.

Butter 75g (3oz), softened
Tomato purée 2 tsp
Chopped dill 2 tbsp, plus a few fronds to garnish
Capers 2–3 tbsp, well drained and roughly chopped
Freshly ground black pepper
Mediterranean-style bread with olives 4 slices, approximately 2cm (¾in) thick, cut diagonally
Eggs 5 large, beaten
Smoked salmon slices 100g packet, cut into thin strips
Beefsteak tomato 1, deseeded and diced, to garnish (optional)

Put 50g (2oz) of the butter into a small bowl, then add the tomato purée, chopped dill and capers. Season with black pepper, then mix well together and set aside.

Toast the bread and keep warm. Melt the remaining butter in a small saucepan (preferably non-stick), add the eggs and half of the salmon strips. Then cook over a moderate heat, stirring continuously, until the eggs are softly scrambled – taking care not to overcook, as they will become dry.

Spread the toasted bread with the tomato butter and put onto two serving plates. Spoon the scrambled eggs on top, garnish with the remaining strips of salmon, dill and the chopped tomato, and serve immediately.

COOK'S TIP
For quick assembly, prepare all the ingredients before starting to cook and toast the bread while scrambling the eggs.

Preparation time	**15 minutes**
Cooking time	**15 minutes**
Calories per portion	**214 Kcal**
Fat per portion	**3g**
of which saturated	**0.4g**
Serves	**4**

Super speedy seafood stew

A deliciously light combination of seafood simmered in a fragrant tomato sauce.

Red pepper 1, deseeded and chopped
Yellow pepper 1, deseeded and chopped
Onion 1 large, peeled and chopped
Garlic 1 clove, peeled and crushed
Bay leaf 1
Rosemary 1 large sprig
Thyme a few sprigs
Coriander seeds 2 tsp, lightly crushed
Dry white wine 200ml (7fl oz)
Chopped tomatoes 400g can
Fish or vegetable stock 200ml (7fl oz)
Courgette 1 large, trimmed and chopped
Prepared cooked seafood 400g packet
Caster sugar 2 tsp
Salt and freshly ground black pepper
Chopped parsley 2 tbsp

Put the peppers, onion and garlic in a large saucepan. Add the herbs and coriander seeds. Pour in the wine, bring to the boil, cover and simmer for 5 minutes, until softened.

Stir in the tomatoes, stock and courgette. Bring to the boil, then simmer gently, uncovered, for a further 5 minutes.

Stir in the seafood, sugar and seasoning. Heat through over a low heat, stirring, for about 5 minutes until piping hot. Discard the herbs and serve ladled into warmed bowls, sprinkled with chopped parsley. Accompany with crusty bread to mop up the sauce.

COOK'S TIP
You can use small chunks of firm white fish fillet (such as pollock, haddock or cod) for this recipe instead of the seafood. Simply add to the sauce and cook for about 5 minutes.

SAUCEPAN

Preparation time	**5 minutes**
Cooking time	**25 minutes**
Calories per portion	**410 Kcal**
Fat per portion	**22g**
of which saturated	**10.5g**
Serves	**4**

Stuffed chicken with bacon

Moist and creamy chicken with a special sauce.

Goats' cheese 110g (4oz)
Chicken breasts 4, skin on
Olive oil 1 tbsp
Smoked streaky bacon rashers 4
Butter 25g (1oz)
Chestnut mushrooms 250g (9oz), wiped and sliced
Plain flour 1 tbsp
White wine 250ml (9fl oz)
Chicken stock cube ½ cube, crumbled
Salt and freshly ground black pepper

Divide the goats' cheese into four and push a portion under the skin of each of the chicken breasts. Heat the oil in a large saucepan and add the chicken breasts, skin side down.

Cook for 4–5 minutes over a medium heat until the chicken skins are golden in colour. Turn the chicken over and cook for a further 3–4 minutes. Remove from the pan.

Add the bacon to the pan and cook for 2–3 minutes, then remove and set aside.

Add the butter to the pan and heat until foaming, then add the sliced mushrooms. Cook for 2–3 minutes until the mushrooms have started to soften, then stir in the flour.

Gradually stir in the wine and 100ml (3½fl oz) water, allowing the mixture to come to the boil between each addition of liquid. Stir in the crumbled stock cube.

Cut the bacon rashers in half and return to the pan with the chicken, skin side up. Cook for a further 10–15 minutes, or until the chicken is cooked through. Season to taste before serving with a Dressed leaves salad (see page 7).

COOK'S TIP
Take care when adding salt to this recipe – the cheese and bacon are both salty.

Preparation time	25 minutes
Cooking time	20 minutes
Calories per portion	304 Kcal
Fat per portion	4g
of which saturated	0.7g
Serves	2

Meatballs with noodles

Meatballs and crunchy vegetables on noodles suffused with delicate flavours.

For the meatballs

Minced turkey or chicken breast 250g (9oz)
Thai red chilli 1, deseeded and finely diced
Finely grated root ginger ½ tsp
Thai fish sauce 1 tsp
Caster sugar a good pinch
Spring onions 2, trimmed and finely chopped
Cornflour 1 level tsp
Chopped coriander leaves 2 tbsp (keep the stalks for the stock)

For the stock

Root ginger a few slivers
Red chilli a few slivers
Garlic 1 clove, halved and lightly crushed
Lemon grass 1 stick, lightly crushed
Dried mushrooms a few (optional)

Thai fish sauce about 1 tbsp
Shiitake mushrooms 50g (2oz), wiped and halved
Celery 1 stick, finely sliced
Spring onions 2, trimmed and finely sliced
Sugar snap peas 75g (3oz), halved lengthways
Straight-to-wok noodles 150g pack
Pak choi 1 head, cut into quarters
Lime 1, juice only
Chopped coriander leaves 2 tbsp

To make the meatballs, mix together all the ingredients for the meatballs (using your hand is best) in a mixing bowl, then divide the mixture into 14 and roll each piece into a small ball. Place the meatballs on a plate, cover with cling film and chill while you make the stock.

For the stock, put the ingredients in a medium-sized saucepan with 1 litre (1¾ pints) cold water. Bring to the boil with the lid on, simmer for 10 minutes, take off the heat and leave until you want to cook the meatballs.

Using a draining spoon, take out and discard the ginger, garlic, lemon grass and any coriander stalks. Leave the dried mushrooms in if you have used them. Reheat the stock in the pan to boiling, add the meatballs and simmer for 3–4 minutes. Remove the meatballs with a draining spoon and put in two hot serving bowls. Keep them warm.

Add the fish sauce, mushrooms, celery, spring onions, sugar snaps and noodles. Bring back to the boil, stir and add the pak choi wedges. Simmer, uncovered, for 2 minutes. Sprinkle with lime juice.

To serve, spoon some of the vegetables and noodles and broth over the meatballs and garnish with roughly torn coriander leaves. Top up with the rest of the broth as second helpings.

COOK'S TIP

Instead of making meatballs, you can cook slices of chicken, slivers of beef or raw prawns in the broth.

49

Preparation time	10 minutes
Cooking time	25 minutes
Calories per portion	527 Kcal
Fat per portion	26g
of which saturated	16.4g
Serves	4

Thai chicken curry with noodles

A fresh and mild curry with a zesty tang.

Vegetable oil 1 tbsp
Thai curry paste 3 tsp
Skinless, boneless chicken thighs 8, each cut into 4 or 6 square-ish pieces
Coconut milk 400ml can
Aubergine 1, cut into 2.5cm (1in) chunks
Baby sweetcorn 10, halved lengthways
Tenderstem broccoli 110g (4oz), cut into 5cm (2in) lengths

Straight-to-wok noodles 300g packet
Lime 1, grated zest and juice
Thai fish sauce 2 tbsp
Coriander good handful of leaves, left whole or chopped
Thai red chillies 1 or 2, deseeded and finely sliced (optional)
Lime wedges (optional)

Heat the oil in large saucepan. Stir in the curry paste and cook for half a minute. Add the chicken pieces and fry gently until sealed.

Stir in the coconut milk then add the aubergine and baby sweetcorn and bring to the boil. Simmer, with the pan half covered, for 10 minutes.

Add the broccoli stems and cook for another 2 minutes. Then stir in the noodles and put the broccoli heads to steam on top of them. Simmer, uncovered, for 3–5 minutes until the vegetables are just tender.

Season with lime zest and juice and add fish sauce, to taste, and whole or chopped coriander leaves, holding some back to garnish.

Stir gently and serve in warmed bowls. Garnish with red chilli, if you like, and a few more coriander leaves and lime wedges, if using, along with the remaining fish sauce for seasoning to personal taste.

COOK'S TIP
If you like a bit more heat in your Thai curry, add some grated root ginger, garlic and sliced chillies along with the curry paste.

Preparation time	10 minutes
Cooking time	30 minutes
Calories per portion	684 Kcal
Fat per portion	23g
of which saturated	12.5g
Serves	4

Suitable for freezing

Tomato, bacon & cheese risotto

A thick, buttery risotto topped with crisp rocket leaves.

Butter 50g (2oz)
Onion 1, peeled and chopped
Garlic 1 clove, peeled and chopped
Smoked back bacon 6 rashers, trimmed and chopped
Arborio rice 400g (14oz)
Dry white wine 150ml (¼ pint)
Hot chicken or vegetable stock 900ml (1½ pints)
Chopped tomatoes 400g can
Freshly ground black pepper
Wild rocket or baby spinach 50g (2oz)
Parmesan cheese shavings 110g (4oz)

Melt the butter in a large saucepan and gently fry the onion, garlic and bacon for 5 minutes, until softened but not browned. Stir in the rice and cook, stirring, for about a minute, until well combined.

In a jug, mix the wine into the stock, add a ladleful to the rice mixture and cook gently, stirring, until absorbed. Continue adding the wine and stock ladle by ladle to the rice until the stock is used and the rice is creamy

Gradually add the chopped tomatoes and cook, stirring, until the risotto becomes thick, but not sticky. Adding the stock and tomatoes will take about 25 minutes to cook and should not be hurried.

Just before serving, season with black pepper. Serve immediately in warmed bowls, topped with rocket or spinach leaves and Parmesan shavings.

COOK'S TIP
If you prefer not to use wine – or don't have any to hand – replace it with extra stock.

Preparation time	10 minutes
Cooking time	35 minutes
Calories per portion	445 Kcal
Fat per portion	10g
of which saturated	2.6g
Serves	4

Spicy pork pasta & beans

Hearty and tasty comfort food – perfect for chilly evenings.

Olive oil 2 tsp
Pork fillet 375g (13oz), trimmed of any visible fat and sinew and cut into 1cm (½in) cubes
Onion 1, peeled and sliced
Green pepper 1, deseeded and sliced
Garlic 2 cloves, peeled and crushed
Red chilli 1, deseeded and finely chopped
Cumin seeds 2 tsp
Passata 500g (1lb 2oz)
Chicken stock 750ml (1¼ pints)
Pasta, e.g. penne 175g (6oz)
Cannellini beans 420g can, drained and rinsed
Chopped parsley 4 tbsp

Heat the oil in a deep saucepan, add the pork and let it colour all over for 5 minutes. Add the onion, green pepper, garlic and chilli and cook for another 5 minutes. Sprinkle cumin seeds into the pan and stir well. Cook for another minute.

Pour in the passata and stock, bring to the boil then add the pasta. Bring it back to the boil and add the beans and half the parsley. Season to taste and stir well.

Cook, uncovered, over a low to medium heat for 15 minutes, stirring occasionally, until the pasta is just tender and coated in a thick sauce (add a little hot water if the sauce gets too thick).

Sprinkle with the rest of the parsley and then let the stew stand for 5 minutes before serving straight from the pot.

COOK'S TIP
With the cumin seeds and chilli this dish could be quite spicy, although this will depend on the chilli. Take the heat out by adding some tomato ketchup or sugar.

Preparation time	5 minutes
Cooking time	25 minutes
Calories per portion	405 Kcal
Fat per portion	20g
of which saturated	7.4g
Serves	4

Suitable for freezing

Beef with winter vegetables

Soft, mellow vegetables and meat flavoured with wine and stock.

Sunflower oil 2 tbsp
Scotch beef frying steak 450g (1lb), cubed
Unsalted butter 25g (1oz)
Shallots 12, trimmed and peeled
Celery 2 sticks, trimmed and sliced
Carrots 2, peeled and sliced
Parsnips 2, peeled and sliced
Plain flour 2 tbsp
Red wine 300ml (½ pint)
Beef stock 300ml (½ pint)
Gravy browning dash (optional)
Chopped thyme 1 tbsp
Salt and freshly ground black pepper

Heat 1 tablespoon of the oil in a large, deep saucepan. Add the beef and cook over a high heat for 4–5 minutes, stirring occasionally. Tip the beef and juices out of the pan onto a plate.

Heat the butter and remaining oil in the pan and add the vegetables. Cook for about 5 minutes until they start to soften.

Add the flour to the pan and stir into the juices. Then gradually add the red wine and beef stock, allowing the mixture to come to the boil between each addition of the liquid.

Return the beef and juices to the pan and stir in a little gravy browning, if using. Stir in the thyme and season to taste.

Cover the pan and simmer for 15–20 minutes until the vegetables and meat are just tender. Serve immediately with crusty bread.

COOK'S TIP
To freeze, pack into a freezer container, seal and freeze for up to 3 months. Allow to defrost in a cool place before reheating.

Preparation time	**40 minutes**
Cooking time	**40 minutes**
Calories per portion	**518 Kcal**
Fat per portion	**24.3g**
of which saturated	**15.1g**
Serves	**6**

Suitable for freezing

Suitable for vegetarians

Cider-soaked fruit

Tangy, gently spiced whole fruit with cream.

Strong, dry cider 1 litre (1¾ pints)
Lemons 3, finely pared rind cut into strips and juice
Oranges 2, finely pared rind cut into strips and juice
Cinnamon stick 15cm (6in) piece
Whole cloves 6–8
Whole cardamom pods 12
Demerara sugar 175g (6oz)
Dessert apples 6, peeled, stalks left on
Ripe pears 6, peeled, stalks left on
Double cream 300ml (½ pint)

Pour the cider into a very large saucepan, add the lemon and orange rind and juice, the spices and sugar. Bring slowly to the boil, stirring occasionally, until the sugar dissolves.

With the tip of a small, pointed knife, remove the calyx from each apple and pear – it is like removing a small cone shape from the base.

Place the apples and pears in the cider, ensuring they are well covered, then cover the pan and cook gently for 35–40 minutes, until translucent and the tip of the knife goes in easily. Gently turn the fruit several times during cooking and do not allow the cider to boil or the fruit will break up.

COOK'S TIP
If serving cold, the apples and pears can be cooked 2–3 days beforehand and stored, covered, in the refrigerator.

When cooked, carefully remove the apples and pears from the cider with a slotted spoon and place in a large serving bowl. Then remove the orange and lemon rind, and the spices, and add to the fruit (keep warm if serving hot).

Bring the cider to the boil and simmer gently until it has reduced by two-thirds and is slightly syrupy. Pour over the fruit and serve with a jug of double cream for pouring over. The pears are delicious hot or leave them to cool, then cover and refrigerate.

Preparation time	**15 minutes**
Cooking time	**5 minutes**
Calories per portion	**351 Kcal**
Fat per portion	**27.6g**
of which saturated	**10g**
Serves	**6**
Suitable for vegetarians	

White chocolate fondue

This is such a fun recipe to try, and the kids will love it too.

White chocolate 225g (8oz)
Double cream 200ml (7fl oz)
Orange 1, ½ tsp finely grated rind and
4 tbsp juice

To serve
Skewers of cubed Jamaican ginger cake, slices of apple, orange, banana, strawberries and marshmallows for dipping

COOK'S TIP
Ring the changes by using dark or milk chocolate instead of the white and look out for varieties that include nuts or pieces of chilli or orange.

Break the chocolate into small pieces and place them in a small saucepan.

Add the cream, orange rind and juice, and heat the mixture very gently, stirring frequently, until the chocolate has melted and warmed through, and the texture is smooth and creamy.

Either serve straight from the saucepan or pour into a heatproof bowl and serve with assorted 'dippers'.

Preparation time	10 minutes
Cooking time	10 minutes
Calories per portion	58 Kcal
Fat per portion	0.4g
of which saturated	0.1g
Serves	4

Suitable for vegetarians

Gingered gooseberry fool

Sharp, fruity fool sweetened with a drizzle of honey.

Gooseberries 250g (9oz), topped and tailed
Root ginger 5mm (¼in) piece, peeled and grated
Honey 3 tbsp
Low fat natural yogurt 75g (3oz)
Egg 1, white only

Tip the gooseberries into a saucepan and add 3–4 tablespoons of water and the ginger and 2 tablespoons of honey. Place the pan over a medium heat and bring to a simmer.

Reduce the heat and let the fruit simmer gently for 5–8 minutes, or until the gooseberries mash to a pulp. Leave the purée to cool then fold the yogurt into the gooseberry purée.

Whisk the egg white until stiff and fold it into the purée. Spoon into serving dishes and serve immediately with the remaining honey drizzled on top.

COOK'S TIP
The gooseberry and ginger purée may be cooked a day or two in advance and kept in the fridge. Eat the fool shortly after making, or the whisked egg whites will collapse.

Wok

The wok is the most important cooking vessel in southeast Asia and China and has become a staple on the equipment rack of many western kitchens.

It is perfect for fast cooking of fresh ingredients while its size and shape allows for the addition of a sauce. It was apparently developed to allow for cooking on bamboo fires, which burn very quickly, and one myth is that the first woks were the upturned shields of Chinese warriors!

Naturally, we have included eastern dishes such as Gingery prawn stir-fry, Five-spice beef with chilli & peppers and Thai fish curry. However, there are interesting variations such as stir-fries of Aubergine & sweet potato or Chicken & asparagus.

Preparation time	**10 minutes**
Cooking time	**25 minutes**
Calories per portion	**336 Kcal**
Fat per portion	**18g**
of which saturated	**3.4g**
Serves	**2**
Suitable for vegetarians	

Aubergine & sweet potato stir-fry

Tender vegetables coated in a sticky sweet glaze.

Sesame oil 2 tbsp
Sweet potato 1, peeled and cut into bite-sized chunks
Aubergine 1, cut into bite-sized chunks
Red onion 1 small, peeled and sliced
Grated root ginger 1 tbsp
Garlic 1 clove, peeled and chopped
Red chilli 1 small, deseeded and finely sliced, or a good pinch of crushed dried chillies
Muscovado sugar 1 tbsp
Soy sauce 2 tbsp
Seasoned rice vinegar or sherry vinegar 2 tbsp
Frozen green beans 200g (7oz), chopped to short, even lengths
Toasted pine nuts small handful
Mint leaves 8–10, shredded if large
Greek yogurt 3 tbsp

Heat a large wok (that has a lid) and, when hot, add the sesame oil and sweet potato chunks and stir-fry for 2 minutes. Add the aubergine and onion slices and cook for another 2 minutes.

Meanwhile, mix the ginger, garlic and chilli in a small bowl with the sugar, soy sauce, rice vinegar and 5 tablespoons warm water.

Pour this mixture into the pan and stir until the vegetables are coated well. Put the lid on and cook for 15 minutes, stirring a few times, until the potato and aubergine are just tender and browned.

Add 2 more tablespoons of warm water and the frozen beans to the pan. Stir and cook for 3 minutes.

Take off the heat and divide between warmed bowls. To serve, sprinkle with the pine nuts, whole or shredded mint leaves and a dollop of yogurt.

COOK'S TIP
If you don't have a lid for your wok, use one from a frying pan. It doesn't matter if it is smaller and fits inside the wok.

Preparation time	20 minutes
Cooking time	10 minutes
Calories per portion	217 Kcal
Fat per portion	15.3g
of which saturated	1.6g
Serves	4

Suitable for vegetarians

Chinese-style Savoy cabbage

Slightly salty and nutty flavours combine in this delicious dish.

Savoy cabbage ½ small cabbage, cored (approximately 350g/12oz)
Cornflour 2 tsp
Vegetable stock 225ml (8fl oz)
Soy sauce 2 tbsp
Tomato paste 1 tbsp
Groundnut oil 3 tbsp
Spring onions 1 bunch, trimmed and sliced diagonally
Garlic 1 clove, peeled and crushed
Water chestnuts 220g can, drained and sliced
Fresh bean sprouts 150g (5oz)
Cashew nuts 50g (2oz)

Cut the cabbage into fine shreds and set aside. Blend together the cornflour, stock, soy sauce and tomato paste in a small bowl and also set aside.

Heat the oil in a large wok, add the spring onions and garlic and stir-fry for 1–2 minutes. Then add the cabbage and continue cooking until cabbage has softened, yet is still slightly crisp.

Add the water chestnuts and bean sprouts to the wok and cook for 1 minute. Stir in the cornflour mixture and bring to the boil. Reduce the heat and cook gently for 1 minute. Scatter the cashew nuts over the cabbage and serve with microwavable rice (cooked as on the packet's instructions).

COOK'S TIP
If you have some sesame oil, then add a little in place of some of the groundnut oil.

63

Preparation time	10 minutes
Cooking time	8 minutes
Calories per portion	723 Kcal
Fat per portion	14g
of which saturated	1.5g
Serves	2

Gingery prawn stir-fry

Crunchy vegetables contrast with juicy prawns.

Vegetable oil 2 tbsp
Garlic 1 clove, peeled and sliced
Root ginger good thumb-sized piece, peeled and cut into slivers
Carrot 1, peeled and cut into thin strips
Runner beans or green beans 110g (4oz), finely sliced
Spring onions 4, trimmed and each cut into 4 pieces
Raw peeled king prawns 200g (7oz)
Thai rice noodles 2 x 125g (3½oz) sheaths
Sherry 4 tbsp
Soy sauce 3 tbsp
Spring greens 1 head 110g (4oz), pulled apart, thick stalk removed, leaves cut into finger-width shreds

Heat the oil in a wok with the garlic and ginger and stir-fry for half a minute. Add the carrot strips and fry for a minute. Stir in the beans, spring onions and prawns and stir-fry for a further 2 minutes. Soak the rice noodles in boiling water as directed on the packet.

Add the sherry and soy sauce, then pour in 250ml (8fl oz) boiling water. Bring to the boil and add the noodles. Bring back to the boil and spread the greens out over the top. Cook for 2 minutes, stirring all the time.

Leave to stand for a minute for the noodles to absorb some more water, then serve straight from the wok. Have the soy sauce and some sesame oil handy on the table for extra seasoning if you like.

COOK'S TIP
Use a small bean slicer gadget for speed and to get the beans all about the same width.

Preparation time	**15 minutes**
Cooking time	**10–15 minutes**
Calories per portion	**334 Kcal**
Fat per portion	**20g**
of which saturated	**14.5g**
Serves	**4**

Thai fish curry

Creamy fragrant broth with two delicious varieties of fish.

Red chillis 2, halved and deseeded
Lemon grass 1 stalk, trimmed and sliced
Shallot 1, peeled and quartered
Garlic 2 cloves, peeled and halved
Root ginger 2.5cm (1in) piece, peeled and sliced
Coriander small handful, plus extra chopped coriander
Lime 1, grated zest only
Fish sauce 1 tbsp
Coconut milk 400ml can
Caster sugar 1 tsp
Sunflower oil 1 tbsp
Monkfish fillet 500g (1lb 2oz), skinned and cubed
Haddock fillet 250g (9oz), cubed

Put the chillis, lemon grass, shallot, garlic, ginger, coriander, lime zest (reserving some to garnish), fish sauce, 6 tablespoons of the coconut milk and sugar in a blender and whizz to make a thick paste.

Heat the oil in a wok and tip in the paste and fry for 2 minutes. Add the remaining coconut milk, bring to a simmer and cook gently for 5 minutes.

Carefully add the fish and coat in the curry paste. Add enough of the remaining coconut to make a sauce and cook until the fish is cooked through. Stir every now and then very gently so the fish doesn't break up.

Serve the curry in small bowls with microwavable fragrant Thai jasmine rice (cooked as on the packet's instructions), garnished with the extra chopped coriander and lime zest.

COOK'S TIP
If you want to make a green Thai curry, use green chillis instead of red. Check the heat of the chillis before using.

Preparation time	10 minutes
Cooking time	9 minutes
Calories per portion	316 Kcal
Fat per portion	9g
of which saturated	1.3g
Serves	2

Lemon & garlic chicken

Sweet and tangy oriental-flavoured chicken with leaves and broccoli.

Skinless, boneless chicken breasts 2, cut into thin strips
Lemon 1, grated zest and juice
Clear honey 2 tsp
Light soy sauce 1 tbsp
Garlic 2 cloves, peeled and finely chopped
Cornflour 4 tsp
Purple sprouting broccoli 8 spears, trimmed
Vegetable oil 1 tbsp
Pak choi 1, trimmed and shredded
Chinese leaves ¼ head, trimmed and shredded
Chives small bunch, snipped

COOK'S TIP
Tender young sprouting broccoli spears are ideal for stir-frying, but use small florets of broccoli when they aren't in season.

Place the chicken strips in a shallow dish. Mix the lemon zest and juice into the chicken along with the honey, soy sauce, garlic and cornflour. Set aside. Cut the broccoli spears into thin, even-sized slices down the length of each piece.

Heat the oil in a wok until hot. Drain the chicken, reserving the juices, and add to the wok; stir-fry for 5 minutes, until well sealed. Add the broccoli and continue to stir-fry for a further 2 minutes.

Finally, add the shredded pak choi, Chinese leaves and reserved juices and stir-fry for a further 2 minutes until the leaves have just wilted. Serve immediately, sprinkled with snipped chives.

Preparation time	8 minutes
Cooking time	35 minutes
Calories per portion	521 Kcal
Fat per portion	18g
of which saturated	7.6g
Serves	4

Chicken tikka pilaff

Tender chicken and peppers in a curry sauce sprinkled with almonds.

Butter 50g (2oz)
Skinless, boneless chicken breasts 3–4, cubed
Tikka curry paste 3–4 level tbsp
Onion 1, peeled and cut into thin wedges
Red pepper 1, deseeded and chopped
Green pepper 1, deseeded and chopped
Basmati rice 250g (9oz)

Boiling water about 600ml (1 pint)
Chicken stock cube 1, crumbled
Spinach 300g (11oz), shredded if large leaves
Chopped coriander 2 tbsp
Salt and freshly ground black pepper
Toasted flaked almonds 1–2 tbsp

Melt the butter in a wok and add the chicken, curry paste and onion. Stir over a medium heat for 5–8 minutes, or until the chicken is cooked, stirring the mixture occasionally. Add the red and green pepper to the wok and cook for a further 2–3 minutes, until the peppers start to soften.

Add the basmati rice to the wok and cook it for 1–2 minutes, stirring it so that the rice is coated in the spice mixture.

Pour the boiling water into the wok and add the stock cube. Reduce the heat, and simmer the mixture for 15–18 minutes, stirring it occasionally so that it does not stick to the pan. If the mixture is looking too dry, then pour in a little more boiling water.

When the rice is just cooked, add the spinach to the wok and cook for a further 1–2 minutes, stirring it continually until the spinach wilts. Stir in the coriander and season to taste. Sprinkle with the almonds just before serving.

COOK'S TIP
If you have the time, stir together the chicken and tikka curry paste and marinate the chicken for a few hours before it is cooked.

Preparation time	**40 minutes**
Cooking time	**20 minutes**
Calories per portion	**507 Kcal**
Fat per portion	**15g**
of which saturated	**2.1g**
Serves	**2**

Chicken & asparagus stir-fry

Intense flavours of soy and orange complement the chicken and noodles.

Skinless, boneless chicken breasts
2, cut in half horizontally and then
diagonally into thin strips
Dark soy sauce 3 tbsp
Large orange 1, grated zest and juice
Corn oil 2 tbsp
Spring onions 150g (5oz), trimmed
and cut into long pieces diagonally
Asparagus 6 large spears, woody
ends removed, stems lightly trimmed
Baby pak choi 4, halved lengthways
Cucumber 150g (5oz) piece, cut into
bite-sized chunks
Straight-to-wok noodles 300g
packet

Put the chicken strips into a bowl,
add the soy sauce and orange zest
and juice and mix together gently.
Cover and leave to marinate for
30 minutes.

Heat the oil in a large wok. Using a
slotted spoon, remove the chicken
strips from the marinade and add
to the wok together with the spring
onions and asparagus.

Stir-fry until the chicken is opaque
and the asparagus is almost tender.
Add the pak choi and cucumber and
continue stir-frying until they, too, are
just tender.

Add the noodles to the wok together
with the reserved marinade, mix into
the chicken and vegetables and then
heat gently for 3–4 minutes, or until
the noodles are hot.

COOK'S TIP
Don't be put off by the idea of hot
cucumber, it is not dissimilar to courgette,
but with a milder, more delicate flavour.

Preparation time	**5 minutes**
Cooking time	**15 minutes**
Calories per portion	**333 Kcal**
Fat per portion	**10g**
of which saturated	**2.4g**
Serves	**4**

Singapore noodles

Sweet and sharp, this stir-fry is packed with flavour, colour and texture.

Sunflower oil 1 tbsp
Pork fillet 150g (5oz), cut into thin strips
Raw tiger prawns 150g (5oz), defrosted if frozen
Spring onions 6, trimmed and sliced
Garlic 1 clove, peeled and crushed
Root ginger 2.5cm (1in) cube, peeled and grated
Stir-fry vegetables 300g ready prepared packet
Sweet chilli dipping sauce 4 tbsp
Soy sauce 2 tbsp
Straight-to-wok noodles 300g packet
Eggs 2, beaten
Lime 1, quartered (optional)

Heat the oil in a large wok and add the pork fillet to the pan. Cook the pork for 4–5 minutes, over a high heat, stirring occasionally, until the meat starts to turn golden in colour. Add the prawns to the wok and cook for a further 2–3 minutes, until the prawns turn pink. Add the spring onions, garlic and ginger and cook for about 1 minute, stirring well so that the garlic does not burn.

Tip the stir-fry vegetables into the wok and cook for 2–3 minutes, over a medium heat, stirring well until the vegetables start to wilt. Add the chilli sauce and soy sauce and stir well to coat the vegetables, then add the noodles and cook for a further 1–2 minutes to heat the noodles.

Use a spatula to move the noodles to one side of the wok and pour the beaten eggs into the clear area. Stir the eggs occasionally so that they set in curds, a little like scrambled egg. Then stir the mixture to incorporate the egg. Serve immediately, with the lime wedges, if using, to squeeze over the noodles.

COOK'S TIP
When buying a ready prepared stir-fry vegetable mix for this recipe, try to choose a packet with beansprouts for texture and with some red pepper to give colour.

Preparation time	**10 minutes**
Cooking time	**8 minutes**
Calories per portion	**285 Kcal**
Fat per portion	**13g**
of which saturated	**3.5g**
Serves	**2**

Five-spice beef with chilli & peppers

Warming and lightly scented, this meaty meal is a treat for the taste buds.

Lean fillet or sirloin steak 225g (8oz), trimmed and cut into very thin strips
Dark soy sauce 1 tbsp
Chinese five-spice powder ½ tsp
Clear honey 2 tsp
Garlic 1 clove, peeled and finely chopped
Small red chilli 1, deseeded and finely chopped
Vegetable oil 1 tbsp
Red pepper 1 small, deseeded and finely sliced
Yellow pepper 1 small, deseeded and finely sliced
Spring onions 1 bunch, trimmed and thinly sliced
Canned water chestnuts 75g (3oz), drained, rinsed and sliced

Place the strips of beef in a shallow dish. Mix with the soy sauce, five-spice powder, honey, garlic and chilli and set aside to marinate.

Heat the oil in a wok until hot and stir-fry the peppers for 3 minutes. Add the beef mixture and the spring onions and continue to stir-fry for 3–4 minutes, until the beef is well sealed.

Add the water chestnuts and stir-fry for a further minute until piping hot. Serve immediately with microwavable rice (cooked as on the packet's instructions).

COOK'S TIP
Chilli adds 'bite' to a recipe, but also a spicy heat. If you prefer less of a 'kick', use a mild green chilli in place of the red chilli.

Preparation time	10 minutes
Cooking time	15 minutes
Calories per portion	733 Kcal
Fat per portion	21g
of which saturated	3.9g
Serves	2

Duck with plum sauce

A bed of noodles with rich and succulent duck breasts and fruity sauce.

For the plum sauce
Red plums 200g (7oz), halved, stoned and quartered
Cinnamon stick 1, halved
Dried red chilli 1, crumbled
Preserving or granulated sugar 75g (3oz) (or to taste)
Red wine vinegar 3 tbsp

For the duck
Olive oil 2 tbsp
Red onion 1, peeled and finely chopped
Root ginger 5cm (2in) piece, peeled and chopped
Skinless, boneless mini duck fillets 225g packet, or larger fillets, sliced
Pak choi 3, trimmed and sliced
Straight-to-wok noodles 300g packet

For the plum sauce, cook the plums in a wok with the cinnamon, chilli and sugar over a gentle heat for a minute or so. Then add the vinegar, stir well and simmer for 5–10 minutes or until the plums are tender and the liquid has reduced. The exact time will depend on the ripeness of the plums. Stir often to prevent the mixture from sticking to the wok. Tip into a bowl and remove the cinnamon stick. Rinse the wok.

To cook the duck, heat the oil in the wok, add the onion and ginger and stir-fry for a minute or so. Then add the duck and stir-fry for about 6 minutes or until the meat is golden and tender. Add the pak choi and noodles and stir-fry for 2 minutes.

Add half the plum sauce, mix well and serve on warm plates with the rest of the plum sauce in a separate bowl.

COOK'S TIP
Oriental food specialists Amoy make great straight-to-wok noodles. After cooking your stir-fry ingredients, you just add to the wok and cook for 1–2 minutes.

Casserole dish

Since prehistoric times, food has been cooked in tightly covered clay vessels hung over the fire. The method softens up fibrous meats, blends in the succulent juices, and allows for the addition of other ingredients such as vegetables to help the dish feed more hungry mouths.

Casserole cooking allows for interesting blends of ingredients, especially meat with fruit, which produces a melting pot of rich flavours and textures. Examples include Chicken & apple, Fruity gammon and Lamb with cherries – the cheaper, fattier cuts of lamb are ideal for casserole dishes. Other succulent slow-cooked combinations in this chapter are Vegetable & barley casserole and Meatballs with butterbeans.

Preparation time	1 hour
Cooking time	30 minutes
Calories per portion	401 Kcal
Fat per portion	24g
of which saturated	8.8g
Serves	4

Suitable for freezing

Suitable for vegetarians if using a Parmesan substitute

Vegetarian moussaka-style bake

Softened Mediterranean vegetables layered with creamy sauce.

Butter 25g (1oz)
Plain flour 25g (1oz)
Milk 600ml (1 pint)
Vegetable stock cube 1
Salt and freshly ground black pepper
Nutmeg for grating (optional)
Aubergines 2 medium–large, trimmed and cut lengthways into strips, 5mm (¼in) thick
Light olive oil 4–6 tbsp

Onions 2 large, peeled and thinly sliced
Garlic 2 cloves, peeled and finely chopped
Courgettes 450g (1lb), trimmed and cut lengthways into long strips, 5mm (¼in) thick
Artichoke hearts 240g can, drained and halved
Chopped tomatoes 400g can, slightly drained
Parmesan cheese 50g (2oz), grated

To make the sauce, melt the butter in a shallow flameproof casserole (approximately 25cm (10in) in diameter and 6cm (2½in) deep). Stir the flour into the butter and add the milk and vegetable stock cube. Slowly bring to the boil, stirring continuously, until the sauce thickens. Season with a little salt, pepper and nutmeg, then pour into a jug, cover the surface with cling film and set aside. Rinse and dry the casserole.

Preheat the oven to 220°C/425°F/Gas 7. Sprinkle the aubergine slices lightly with salt, leave to stand for 10 minutes and then pat dry with kitchen paper. Meanwhile, heat 1 tablespoon of the olive oil in the casserole, add the onions and garlic and cook gently until softened but not browned. Then remove from the pan and set aside.

Heat a little more olive oil in the casserole, then adding a few at time, cook the aubergine slices for 2–3 minutes each side, until lightly browned. Remove from the dish and drain on kitchen paper. Cook the courgettes slices in the same way.

Arrange a single layer of aubergine slices in the bottom of the casserole, add a layer of courgettes, followed by some onions and artichokes and some of the chopped tomatoes, season with black pepper, then drizzle a little of the sauce over the vegetables. Continue layering the vegetables and sauce, ending with a layer of aubergine slices, if possible. Take care not to add too much sauce with each layer as at least half will be needed to pour over the top.

Spread the remaining sauce over the vegetables and then sprinkle the Parmesan evenly over the top. Place the casserole on a baking tray and cook in the oven for about 30 minutes, or until the vegetables are cooked. If the top is browning too quickly, cover with a lid or foil.

COOK'S TIP
A can of chunky tomato soup or a small jar of tomato pasta sauce could also be substituted for the can of tomatoes. For extra flavour, choose a can of tomatoes with added herbs.

Preparation time	25 minutes
Cooking time	1½ hours
Calories per portion	444 Kcal
Fat per portion	14g
of which saturated	6.6g
Serves	4

Suitable for freezing

Suitable for vegetarians

Vegetable & barley casserole

Winter vegetables and barley combine to create a wholesome dish.

Butter 50g (2oz)
Leeks 2, trimmed and sliced
Onion 1, peeled and sliced
Parsnips 2–3, peeled and cut into chunks
Butternut squash 1 small, peeled, deseeded and cut into chunks
Celeriac 1 small, peeled and cut into chunks
Pearl barley 175g (6oz)
Medium cider 600ml (1 pint)
Cider vinegar 1 tbsp
Vegetable stock cubes 2
Salt and freshly ground black pepper

Preheat the oven to 180°C/350°F/ Gas 4. Melt the butter in a flameproof casserole and add the white part of the leeks and the other vegetables and cook them over a medium heat for 5–7 minutes, until softened.

Rinse the pearl barley and then add it to the casserole dish and stir well, to coat in the butter. Pour in the cider, 300ml (½ pint) water and cider vinegar and add the stock cubes. Bring the mixture to the boil, then cover the casserole and place it in the oven.

Cook the casserole in the oven for 1–1¼ hours or until the pearl barley is tender. About 20 minutes before the end, stir in the green slices of leek. If all the liquids are absorbed, then a little extra boiling water can be added.

Stir the casserole and season to taste. Serve the casserole with crusty bread to soak up the juices.

COOK'S TIP
Keep the vegetables fairly chunky. If they are cut too small, they will cook before the pearl barley and will start to go mushy.

Preparation time	15 minutes
Cooking time	1 hour
Calories per portion	488 Kcal
Fat per portion	19.2g
of which saturated	9.9g
Serves	2

Suitable for freezing

Chicken & apple casserole

Creamy comfort food with the perfect blend of ingredients

Butter 25g (1oz)
Chicken breasts 2 x 200g (7oz), skin on
Onion 1, peeled and quartered
Green dessert apples 2, quartered and cored
Chicken stock cube 1
Plain flour 1 tbsp
Extra strong cider 300ml (½ pint)
Sage 1–2 sprigs
Single cream 2–3 tbsp
Wholegrain mustard 1 tsp

Preheat the oven to 180°C/350°F/Gas 4. Heat the butter in a small flameproof casserole, add the chicken and brown lightly all over. Remove from the casserole and set aside.

Brown the onion and apple in the fat remaining in the casserole, crumble in the stock cube, stir in the flour, add the cider and bring to the boil, stirring.

Return the chicken to the casserole and add the sage. Cover the surface with greaseproof paper, then cover with the lid and cook in the oven for 1 hour. Just before serving, blend the cream with the mustard and drizzle over the chicken.

COOK'S TIP
You may need to add more liquid to the casserole to prevent it drying out – check after 40 minutes.

Preparation time	15 minutes
Cooking time	40 minutes
Calories per portion	603 Kcal
Fat per portion	48g
of which saturated	23.9g
Serves	4
Suitable for freezing	

Chicken with tarragon

Delicate tarragon combined with chicken and cream.

Olive oil 2 tbsp
Shallots 2, peeled, halved and thinly sliced
Garlic 1–2 cloves, peeled and crushed
Shiitake mushrooms 120g punnet, wiped and sliced
Closed cup mushrooms 250g punnet, wiped and sliced
Skinless, boneless chicken breasts 4
White wine 150ml (¼ pint)
Double cream 300ml (½ pint)
Chopped tarragon 2 tbsp, plus extra for garnish
Salt and freshly ground black pepper
Focaccia bread 4 slices, toasted

Heat half the oil in a large, flameproof casserole and cook the shallots, garlic and mushrooms for 5 minutes or until softened. Remove from the pan with a slotted spoon. Add the chicken breasts to the casserole with the remaining oil and cook for about 10 minutes, or until golden.

Add the wine to the casserole and bring to the boil, reduce the heat and simmer for 5–10 minutes, or until reduced by half. Add the cream with the reserved mushroom mixture and tarragon and bring to the boil, reduce the heat and simmer for 15–20 minutes, or until the chicken is cooked through and the creamy sauce is thickened and reduced. Stir every now and then.

Season with salt and pepper to taste and serve the creamy chicken on the toasted focaccia bread with a Creamy dressed leaves salad (see page 7).

COOK'S TIP
If you can't find the specified mushrooms, then use the same amount of oyster or field mushrooms, wiped and sliced.

Preparation time	**30 minutes**
Cooking time	**1¼ hours**
Calories per portion	**733 Kcal**
Fat per portion	**35.7g**
of which saturated	**14g**
Serves	**4**
Suitable for freezing	

Fruity gammon casserole

A melting pot of rich flavours and meaty textures.

COOK'S TIP
Instead of single cream and parsley, finish the dish with 2 tablespoons of crème fraîche and chopped chives or a mix of finely chopped parsley, rosemary and thyme leaves.

Unsmoked gammon joint approximately 680g (1½lb)
Butter 50g (2oz)
Button onions or shallots 12, peeled
Baby potatoes 350g (12oz), scrubbed
Baby carrots 350g (12oz), scrubbed
Flour 2 tbsp
Chicken stock 350ml (12fl oz)
Strong cider 300ml (½ pint)
Herbs 1 sprig parsley, rosemary, thyme and bay leaf
Broad beans 225g (8oz), fresh or frozen
Pitted prunes 12 large
Cox's apples 4 whole, cored
Single cream 4 tbsp
Chopped flat-leaved parsley

Preheat the oven to 180°C/350°F/Gas 4. Cut the rind and excess fat from the gammon. Cut the meat from the bone and then cut it into 2.5cm (1in) cubes.

Heat the butter in a flameproof casserole, add the gammon and cook until browned. Add the onions, potatoes and carrots, cook for 2–3 minutes and stir in the flour. Then stir in the stock and cider and bring to the boil. Add the herbs, cover with greaseproof paper and then with the lid or some foil and cook for about 1¼ hours.

After 1 hour, add the beans, prunes and apples. Return to the oven until the vegetables are cooked, then remove from the oven, stir in the cream, sprinkle with parsley – and serve.

Preparation time	10 minutes
Cooking time	3¾ hours
Calories per portion	453 Kcal
Fat per portion	26g
of which saturated	9.4g
Serves	4
Suitable for freezing	

Dorset jugged steak

A rich port and redcurrant sauce enhances the slow-cooked beef.

Stewing steak 680g (1½lb), cut into 2.5cm (1in) cubes
Plain wholemeal flour 2 tbsp
Onion 1, peeled and sliced
Cloves 4
Salt and freshly ground black pepper
Port 150ml (¼ pint)
Beef stock 450ml (¾ pint)
Sausagemeat 225g (8oz)
Wholemeal breadcrumbs 50g (2oz)
Chopped parsley 2 tbsp
Redcurrant jelly 1 tbsp

COOK'S TIP
For a cheaper dish, use bitter or light ale in place of the port.

Preheat the oven to 170°C/325°F/Gas 3. Coat the meat with the flour, shaking off any excess, and put into a casserole dish. Add the onion and cloves and season.

Pour the port into the casserole dish and add just enough stock to cover the meat. Cover and bake in the oven for 2¾ hours.

Meanwhile, mix together the sausagemeat, breadcrumbs and parsley and season. With floured hands, shape the sausagemeat into eight balls.

Stir the redcurrant jelly into the casserole and add the sauagemeat balls. Cook, uncovered, for a further 40–45 minutes until the sausagemeat is cooked and slightly browned. Serve hot with thick slices of rustic wholemeal bread.

Preparation time	**20 minutes**
Cooking time	**1 hour 20 minutes**
Calories per portion	**401 Kcal**
Fat per portion	**26g**
of which saturated	**8.3g**
Serves	**4**
Suitable for freezing	

Paprika sausage supper

The tangy crunch of dill pickle provides a delicious contrast to this goulash-style dish.

Good-quality pork sausages 8
Onions 2 large, peeled, each cut into
6 lengthways
Garlic 2–3 cloves, peeled and crushed
Green peppers 2, deseeded and
thickly sliced
Sweet paprika 1 tbsp
Plain flour 1 tbsp
Chicken stock 300ml (½ pint)
Chopped tomatoes 400g can
Soured cream
Sliced dill pickled cucumbers cut
into thin strips
Chopped parsley

Preheat the oven to 180ºC/350ºF/
Gas 4. Heat a large flameproof
casserole and cook the sausages until
they are lightly browned. Remove and
set aside.

Add the onions, garlic and peppers
to the pan and cook them gently until
they are slightly softened. Then stir in
the paprika, flour, stock and tomatoes
and bring to the boil.

Return the sausages to the pan, coat
well with sauce and cover the surface
with greaseproof paper.

Cover the pan with its lid, then
cook in the oven for 1–1¼ hours.
Before serving, skim off the excess
fat. Top with soured cream, dill pickled
cucumbers and parsley and serve
immediately with thick slices of a
French loaf for mopping up the juices.

COOK'S TIP
Supermarkets sell a wide range of flavoured
sausages. Garlicky Toulouse sausages,
chillied sausages, or venison sausages could
also be used for a stronger tasting dish.

Preparation time	**20 minutes**
Cooking time	**2¾ hours**
Calories per portion	**545 Kcal**
Fat per portion	**35g**
of which saturated	**16.2g**
Serves	**4**
Suitable for freezing	

Preparation time	**15 minutes**
Cooking time	**2¼ hours, plus 10 minutes standing**
Calories per portion	**524 Kcal**
Fat per portion	**20g**
of which saturated	**8.8g**
Serves	**4**

Slow-cooked Greek lamb

Savour the scents of Greece with this aromatic, herby lamb roast.

Half leg of lamb approximately 1.1kg (2lb 7oz), trimmed of excess fat
Garlic 6 cloves, peeled and halved
Salt and freshly ground black pepper
Onions 2, peeled and sliced
Rosemary, thyme and oregano a few sprigs
Bay leaves 2
Potatoes 680g (1½lb), peeled and cut into pieces about 2.5cm (1in) thick
Vine tomatoes 4 large, roughly chopped
Pitted dry black olives 50g (2oz)

Preheat the oven to 170°C /325°F/ Gas 3. Using a small sharp knife, stab the flesh of the lamb evenly all over 12 times and insert a piece of garlic into each hole. Season all over.

Put the onions in the bottom of a large casserole dish and sprinkle with the herbs. Sit the lamb on top, pushing it down into the onions and herbs. Cover the top of the dish with foil and then sit the lid on top. Place in the oven.

After 1 hour's cooking, remove the lid and foil, lift out the lamb and put on a heatproof plate. Mix the potatoes and tomatoes into the casserole. Replace the lamb and re-cover. Cook for a further hour, or until tender. For the last 15 minutes, remove the lid and foil, stir the potatoes and sauce and return to the oven for the lamb to brown.

Stir in the olives and allow to stand, covered, for 10 minutes before carving. Discard the herbs and serve with Bean salad (see page 7).

COOK'S TIP
Four spare rib pork chops could also be cooked in this way, but rather than stabbing and inserting with garlic, simply chop and scatter over the pork.

Preparation time	10 minutes
Cooking time	1½ hours
Calories per portion	309 Kcal
Fat per portion	8g
of which saturated	3.5g
Serves	4
Suitable for freezing	

Eastern lamb & apricots

Gently spiced lamb and apricots with fluffy couscous.

Olive oil 1 tbsp
Lean lamb 350g (12oz), diced
Onion 1, peeled and sliced
Ground cinnamon 1 tsp
Ground turmeric 1 tsp
Leek 1, washed and sliced
Red peppers 2, deseeded and
roughly chopped
Ready-to-eat dried apricots 150g
(5oz)
Lemon 1, grated zest and strained
juice
Lamb stock 450ml (¾ pint)
Couscous 110g (4oz)
Chopped flat-leaved parsley 2 tbsp

COOK'S TIP
This recipe is very versatile – it may also
be cooked in a moderate oven rather than
on the hob.

Heat the olive oil in a flameproof casserole dish. Add the lamb and onion to the pan in a single layer. Cook over a high heat, turning occasionally until the lamb is browned on all sides. Add the cinnamon and turmeric and cook for a further minute, stirring well.

Add the leek, red pepper, apricots and lemon zest and juice to the casserole dish and mix with the meat. Pour the stock into the dish. Bring to the boil, then reduce the heat, cover the pan and leave to simmer gently for 1¼–1½ hours, or until the lamb is tender.

Add the couscous, stir and re-cover the pan. Continue to cook for 3–5 minutes, over a gentle heat until the couscous is just tender and the juices thickened. Stir the parsley into the mixture. Serve with a Fruit and nuts salad (see page 7).

Preparation time	15 minutes
Cooking time	1¾ hours
Calories per portion	761 Kcal
Fat per portion	39g
of which saturated	7.9g
Serves	4

Suitable for freezing

Crusted lamb casserole

The pastry topping crumbles to reveal its tasty contents.

For the casserole
Sunflower oil 2 tbsp
Diced lamb 450g (1lb)
Carrots 2, peeled and cut into chunks
Parsnips 2, peeled and cut into chunks
Leeks 2, trimmed and sliced
Plain flour 1 tbsp
New potatoes 500g (1lb 2oz), halved if large
Chopped rosemary 1 tbsp, plus extra for garnish
Lamb stock cube 1
Worcestershire sauce 1 tbsp
Salt and freshly ground black pepper

For the crust
Self-raising flour 175g (6oz)
Salt a pinch
Shredded vegetable suet 75g (3oz)
Egg 1, lightly beaten

COOK'S TIP
As soon as the crust is placed on top of the casserole, return it to the oven otherwise the suet will start to melt from the heat of the mixture.

Preheat the oven to 180°C/350°F/Gas 4. To make the filling, heat the oil in a large flameproof casserole and then add the lamb and cook it for 4–5 minutes, turning it occasionally until it browns on all sides. Add the carrots, parsnips, leeks and potatoes to the pan and cook for a further 4–5 minutes, stirring occasionally.

Sprinkle the flour into the pan and stir to mix it well, then pour in 500ml (18fl oz) water and add the rosemary, stock cube, Worcestershire sauce and seasoning. Bring the contents of the casserole to the boil, stirring continually, then cover the casserole and place it in the oven for 1 hour.

To make the crust, put the flour, salt and suet into a bowl. Add approximately 75–115ml (3–4fl oz) water, or enough to give a firm dough, then flatten the dough out so it is roughly the same size as the top of the casserole, either stretching it out by hand or using a rolling pin.

After the casserole has been in the oven for an hour, take it out and lay the crust on top, brush with beaten egg and then return to the oven. Bake for 20–30 minutes, or until the crust has risen and is a golden colour.

Remove the casserole from the oven, and serve immediately, with extra Worcestershire sauce, if liked, and garnished with chopped rosemary.

Preparation time	**20 minutes**
Cooking time	**1 hour**
Calories per portion	**453 Kcal**
Fat per portion	**21g**
of which saturated	**7.2g**
Serves	**4**

Meatballs with butterbeans

Sweet paprika and peppers give this dish a typical Hungarian goulash flavour.

Extra lean, quality minced beef
500g (1lb 2oz)
Onions 3 small, peeled and finely
chopped
Mixed dried herbs 2 tsp
Sweet paprika 2 tsp
Fresh white breadcrumbs 6 tbsp
Olive oil 3 tbsp
**Salt and freshly ground black
pepper**
Butter 25g (1oz)
Green pepper 1 large, deseeded and
chopped
Red pepper 1 large, deseeded and
chopped
Garlic 2 cloves, peeled and crushed
Chopped tomatoes 400g can
Sugar 1 tsp
Butterbeans 400g can, drained and
rinsed
Basil large bunch

COOK'S TIP
Minced lamb, pork or turkey could
also be used in place of the minced
beef for a change.

Preheat the oven to 180°C/350°F/Gas 4. Place the beef in a large mixing bowl
and add one-third of the chopped onion along with the herbs, paprika, breadcrumbs and 1 tablespoon of the oil.

Season well and mix together thoroughly. Divide the mixture into 12 equal-
sized pieces and shape into balls.

Heat the butter and 1 tablespoon of the oil in a large flameproof casserole, add
the meatballs and fry until lightly browned all over, taking care not to break them
up as you turn them over. Remove from the casserole and set aside.

Heat the remaining oil in the casserole, add the peppers and remaining onion
and cook gently until slightly softened. Mix in the garlic, tomatoes, sugar and
butterbeans and season.

Carefully place the meatballs in the sauce, spooning it over as you do so.
Bring to the boil, then cover with a tight-fitting lid and cook in the oven for 1
hour. Just before serving, finely shred and stir in the basil. Crusty bread and a
Dressed leaves salad (see page 7) make good accompaniments to this dish.

Preparation time	20 minutes
Cooking time	1¾ hours
Calories per portion	670 Kcal
Fat per portion	41g
of which saturated	16.1g
Serves	4

Suitable for freezing

Bacon-wrapped beef

Tender beef parcels containing a light herb and bacon stuffing.

Rindless streaky bacon 75g (3oz), finely chopped, plus 8 rashers
Onions 3, 1 peeled and finely chopped, 2 peeled and sliced
Chopped parsley 2 tsp, plus sprig for garnish
Breadcrumbs 110g (4oz)
Shredded beef suet 50g (2oz)
Dried mixed herbs ¼ tsp
Egg 1
Lemon ½, grated zest and 1 tsp juice
Salt and freshly ground black pepper
Beef 8 slices cut from a joint of topside
English mustard 1 tbsp
Plain flour 3 tbsp
Butter 25g (1oz)
Vegetable oil 2 tbsp
Beef stock 750ml (1¼ pints)

Preheat the oven to 170°C/325°F/Gas 3. Mix the chopped bacon with the finely chopped onion, parsley, breadcrumbs, suet, herbs and egg. Add the lemon zest and juice and seasoning.

Beat each piece of meat with a meat mallet or rolling pin and spread with mustard. Divide the stuffing into eight and place on top of each piece of meat. Roll up, wrap with a rasher of bacon and secure with string.

Season the flour and coat each meat parcel. Heat the butter and oil in a large, shallow, flameproof casserole dish and brown the meat. Remove the meat and keep warm.

Stir the remaining flour into the pan and brown lightly. Slowly add the stock, stirring continuously, and bring to the boil. Return the meat to the casserole.

Scatter the sliced onions over the meat, cover and bake for 1½ hours, until tender. Garnish with parsley and serve with a Bean salad (see page 7).

COOK'S TIP
If you prefer, you can buy a packet mix of stuffing, rather than buy all the stuffing ingredients separately.

Preparation time **20 minutes**

Cooking time **1 hour 50 minutes**

Calories per portion **573 Kcal**

Fat per portion **26g**

of which saturated **4.7g**

Serves **4**

Suitable for freezing

Beef & mushroom casserole with garlic bread crust

The garlicky buttered crust contrasts with the full-bodied beef stew.

Plain flour 4 tsp
Salt and freshly ground black pepper
Lean braising steak 680g (1½lb), trimmed and cut into 1cm (½in) thick pieces
Vegetable oil 2 tbsp
Onions 2, peeled and sliced
Garlic 2 cloves, peeled and crushed
Red wine 250ml (9fl oz)

Beef stock 250ml (9fl oz)
Bay leaf 1
Green beans 150g (5oz), stalks removed and halved
Chestnut mushrooms 150g (5oz), wiped, stalks removed and mushrooms sliced thickly
Loaf chilled garlic bread 1, sliced

Preheat the oven to 180°C/350°F/Gas 4. Place the flour on a plate and season well. Toss the steak pieces in the seasoned flour until well coated.

Heat the oil in a large flameproof casserole and gently fry the onions and garlic for 5 minutes, until just softened. Add the steak with all the flour and cook, stirring, for 5 minutes, until the meat is browned and sealed all over.

Pour in the wine and stock and add the bay leaf. Bring the sauce to the boil, cover and remove from the heat. Put in the oven and cook for 1½ hours. Increase the oven temperature to 200°C/400°F/Gas 6 and stir the green beans and mushrooms into the beef stew. Remove the bay leaf.

Arrange the garlic bread slices in a single layer on top, butter side up, and return to the oven to cook for a further 20 minutes without the lid until the beef is tender and the bread is crisp and lightly golden. Serve immediately.

COOK'S TIP
Chestnut or brown mushrooms are a good choice for casseroling as they are meaty and retain a firm texture, but you can use white mushrooms or field mushrooms if unavailable.

Preparation time	15 minutes
Cooking time	40 minutes
Calories per portion	355 Kcal
Fat per portion	15g
of which saturated	6.5g
Serves	6

Bolognese bake

Traditional Bolognese with a pesto twist.

Minced beef 500g (1lb 2oz)
Onion 1, peeled and chopped
Garlic 2 cloves, peeled and finely chopped
Mushrooms 250g (9oz), wiped and sliced
Chopped tomatoes 400g can
Tomato purée 1 tbsp
Beef stock cubes 2
Boiling water 900ml (1½ pints)
Macaroni 225g (8oz)
Salt and freshly ground black pepper
Green pesto sauce 1–2 tbsp
Worcestershire sauce a dash
Basil leaves handful
Parmesan cheese shavings

Preheat the oven to 200°C/400°F/Gas 6. Place the beef in a large flameproof casserole and cook over a medium heat, stirring occasionally until the fat starts to run out of the meat. Add the onion and garlic to the casserole and cook over a medium heat for about 5 minutes, stirring occasionally, until the onion starts to soften. Then add the sliced mushrooms and cook for a further 3–4 minutes.

Stir in the chopped tomatoes, tomato purée, stock cubes and boiling water and bring the mixture to the boil. Add the pasta and stir to mix well. Cover the casserole dish and place it in the centre of the oven.

Cook for 20 minutes, then take it out of the oven and remove the lid. Stir the mixture well and return it to the oven, uncovered, for a further 10 minutes, or until the pasta is tender.

Remove from the oven and stir in seasoning and then the pesto and Worcestershire sauces to taste. Serve with scattered basil leaves and some Parmesan cheese scattered over the top.

COOK'S TIP
Minced lamb can be used instead of beef, just change the stock cubes, too, using lamb stock cubes or vegetable ones.

Baking dish

Cooking in a baking dish means you can serve it straight from the oven, allowing your family and friends to savour the wonderful food that is just about to be placed in front of them.

Baked dishes can include classics such as pies – there are fish, chicken and ham recipes here – while cheese can be a wonderful ingredient as it melts and disperses its flavour. Examples of these include Creamy cheese & tomato cannelloni, Gruyère, bacon & potato gratin and Pimiento & brie bake. Vegetable dishes such as Moroccan stuffed tomatoes and Baked butternut squash show the versatility of this cooking method. It also suits puddings, such as a wonderful variation on the traditional crumble using blueberries, Cherry bread pudding and the German classic featuring stuffed apples – Bratapfel.

Preparation time	20 minutes
	plus soaking
Cooking time	35 minutes
Calories per portion	136 Kcal
Fat per portion	3g
of which saturated	0.2g
Serves	4
Suitable for vegetarians	

Moroccan stuffed tomatoes

Naturally sweet beefsteak tomatoes, stuffed with fragrant couscous.

Couscous 100g (3½oz)
Large beefsteak tomatoes 4
Red onion 1, peeled and finely chopped
Lemon juice 1 tbsp
Olive oil 1 tsp
Cooked chickpeas 110g (4oz)
Ground cinnamon 1 tsp
Ground cumin 1 tsp
Chopped coriander 3 tbsp
Salt and freshly ground black pepper

Preheat the oven to 190°C/375°F/ Gas 5. Soak the couscous in a large bowl, according to the packet's instructions.

Slice the tops off the tomatoes and scoop out and reserve the pulp and seeds. Stand the tomatoes upside down on kitchen paper to absorb some of the liquid. Set aside. Chop the tomato pulp, discarding the core.

Drain off the excess juice and add the pulp to the bowl of couscous. Then add the onion, lemon juice, chickpeas, spices and coriander, mix together and season to taste.

Pack the couscous mixture into the tomato shells and replace the tomato tops. Stand in a small baking dish and pour in just enough water to cover the bottom of the dish. Cover with foil and bake for 20 minutes. Remove the foil and bake for a further 10 minutes until tender. Drain and serve immediately.

COOK'S TIP
This couscous filling is just as tasty when used to stuff other vegetables, such as peppers, courgettes or aubergines.

Preparation time	**10 minutes**
Cooking time	**1 hour**
Calories per portion	**231 Kcal**
Fat per portion	**7g**
of which saturated	**3.6g**
Serves	**2**

Suitable for vegetarians if using a Parmesan substitute

Baked butternut squash

Meltingly tender squash with a creamy fluffy centre.

Butternut squash 1
Half fat crème fraîche 3 tbsp
Paprika 1 tsp, plus extra for sprinkling
Spring onions 3, trimmed and finely chopped
Grated Parmesan cheese 2 tbsp
Coarse breadcrumbs 2 tbsp

Preheat the oven to 200°C/400°F/Gas 6. Halve the squash lengthways and scoop out the seeds and threads with a spoon and discard them. Put in a baking dish and roast for 40–50 minutes until the flesh is soft when you test it with a knife.

Put the squash halves on a board and leave until cool enough to handle (or put on thick rubber gloves to hold the hot vegetable and do it straightaway). Scrape the flesh into a bowl, leaving a thin border and keeping the skin and shape of the squash intact.

Roughly mash the flesh with a fork and mix with the crème fraîche, paprika and spring onions.

Pile the mixture back into the shells. Put on the baking dish and sprinkle with the grated cheese and breadcrumbs and a little more paprika. Put the squash shells back in the oven and cook for another 10–15 minutes until browned on top and piping hot.

COOK'S TIP
If the squash skin collapses, scrape out all the flesh and pile the mixture into two small, or one larger, gratin dishes for serving – it will taste just as good.

Preparation time	**20 minutes, plus 30 minutes standing**
Cooking time	**20 minutes**
Calories per portion	**544 Kcal**
Fat per portion	**35g**
of which saturated	**18.6g**
Serves	**4**

Suitable for vegetarians if using a Parmesan substitute

Pimiento & brie bake

The stark contrast between fiery pimientos and creamy Brie works wonderfully.

Butter 25g (1oz), softened
Parmesan cheese 75g (3oz)
Plain flour 75g (3oz)
Eggs 4
Milk 600ml (1 pint)
Dijon mustard 2 tsp
Salt and freshly ground black pepper
Whole red pimientos 400g can, drained
Brie 200g (7oz), cubed
Basil leaves small handful, torn

Preheat the oven to 190°C/375°F/ Gas 5. Generously grease a baking dish with the butter. Scatter over half the Parmesan cheese, tipping out any excess. Chill the dish.

Meanwhile, make the batter by whizzing the flour, eggs, milk, mustard and plenty of seasoning in a food processor until smooth. Leave to rest for 30 minutes.

Slice the pimientos into strips and arrange in the dish. Pour over the batter and then sprinkle with the cubes of Brie, basil leaves and remaining Parmesan. Bake in the oven for 20–30 minutes until puffed and golden. Serve immediately with a Refreshing salsa (see page 7).

COOK'S TIP
For a stronger tasting cheese, try with cubed goats' cheese or Camembert. Or a mix of Brie and Dolcelatte or oddments left from a cheeseboard.

Preparation time	**15 minutes**
Cooking time	**40 minutes**
Calories per portion	**300 Kcal**
Fat per portion	**17g**
of which saturated	**6.3g**
Serves	**6**
Suitable for freezing	

Creamy cheese & tomato cannelloni

A bit different, this cannelloni has anchovies and refreshing pesto for extra flavour.

For the sauce
Dried oregano 2 tsp
Sugar 2 tsp
Salt and freshly ground black pepper
Chopped tomatoes 400g can

For the lasagne
Fresh lasagne sheets 12 (300g/11oz pack)
Ricotta cheese 250g tub, softened
Green pesto sauce 6 tbsp
Marinated and grilled red and yellow peppers 200g tub
Baby plum (or cherry) tomatoes 250g (9oz), halved
Canned anchovies 50g (2oz), halved lengthways, reserve oil
Grated Parmesan cheese 4 tbsp
Basil leaves

COOK'S TIP
Use a good quality fresh pesto from a tub on the deli counter and get the peppers from there, too, if you can.

Preheat the oven to 220°C/425°F/Gas 7. Lightly oil a shallow baking dish.

Make the sauce by mixing the oregano, sugar and seasoning (but don't use too much salt because of the anchovies) into the can of tomatoes. Pour half of it into the dish.

Lay the lasagne sheets on the worksurface, six at a time, and roughly spread the ricotta cheese over each one, then spread half a tablespoon of pesto on top and place one or two pieces of pepper at one short end.

Roll up each lasagne sheet from this end and pack them fairly close together in the sauce in the dish. Repeat with the second batch and spoon the rest of the tomato sauce over the top.

Spread the tomato halves over the tomato sauce and arrange anchovy strips on top. Sprinkle with the anchovy oil. Cover with foil and bake for 20 minutes. Remove the foil, sprinkle with Parmesan cheese and bake for a further 20 minutes to brown the cheese. Leave to stand for about 5 minutes before serving.

Scatter with basil leaves and serve with a Fruit and nuts salad (see page 7) and some chunky bread, if you like.

101

Preparation time	15 minutes
Cooking time	15 minutes
Calories per portion	310 Kcal
Fat per portion	12g
of which saturated	4.9g
Serves	4

Stuffed baked trout

Nutty bulghar wheat with lemon zing works well with the delicate flavour of trout.

Bulghar wheat 75g (3oz)
Cucumber 2.5cm (1in) piece
Spring onions 2
Ripe tomato 1
Mint a small bunch
Lemons 2
Whole trout 4 x 225g (8oz)
Salt and freshly ground black pepper
Bay leaves 4
Butter 25g (1oz)

Preheat the oven to 230°C/450°F/ Gas 8. Place the bulghar wheat in a heatproof bowl and cover with boiling water. Stand for 10 minutes.

Meanwhile, finely chop the cucumber. Trim and finely chop the spring onions. Finely chop the tomato. Reserving a few sprigs of mint for garnish, roughly chop the remainder. Finely grate the zest and extract the juice from 1 lemon.

Wash and pat dry the trout and season inside. Drain the bulghar wheat well, and mix with the chopped vegetables, mint, lemon zest and plenty of seasoning. Pack this mixture into the centre of each trout.

Place the trout in a shallow baking dish lined with baking parchment and lay a bay leaf on each fish. Sprinkle with lemon juice and top each trout with a knob of butter. Bake the fish in the oven for 15 minutes, until tender and cooked through.

Drain the trout and discard the bay leaves. Serve sprinkled with the remaining mint, roughly chopped, accompanied with warmed, lightly toasted pitta breads, some crisp salad leaves and wedges of fresh lemon to squeeze over.

COOK'S TIP
In place of the bulghar wheat, use couscous or cooked rice.

Preparation time	10 minutes
Cooking time	20 minutes
Calories per portion	726 Kcal
Fat per portion	61g
of which saturated	11.1g
Serves	2

Baked salmon tricolore

A colourful combination with a summery Mediterranean flavour.

Firm avocado 1 large
Lemon juice 1 tbsp
Tomatoes 2 large, thickly sliced
Olive oil 2 tbsp
Salt and freshly ground black pepper
Salmon fillets 2 x 150g (5oz)
Garlic mayonnaise 2 tbsp
Grated Parmesan cheese 3 tbsp
Chopped basil 2 tbsp
Rocket leaves

Preheat the oven to 200°C/400°F/Gas 6. Line a baking dish with baking parchment.

Cut the avocado in half and prise out the stone. Peel off the skin and then slice thickly. Arrange in a single layer in the baking dish. Sprinkle with lemon juice. Put the tomatoes in the dish and drizzle with half the oil. Season well.

Wash and pat dry the fish. Mix the mayonnaise with the Parmesan cheese and chopped basil. Lay the fish on top of the avocado and tomatoes and spread the mayonnaise mixture on top of the fish. Then drizzle with the remaining oil.

Bake the salmon in the oven for about 20 minutes, depending on the thickness of the fish, until cooked through and tender. Drain and serve immediately with fresh rocket leaves.

COOK'S TIP
Choose a slightly under-ripe avocado for this recipe – it will be easier to peel and slice; the flesh will soften slightly on baking.

Preparation time	15 minutes
Cooking time	30 minutes
Calories per portion	625 Kcal
Fat per portion	47g
of which saturated	22.7g
Serves	4

Fish pie

Succulent salmon with a filo and sesame topping.

Butter 50g (2oz)
Leek 1, trimmed and finely sliced
Frozen sweetcorn and frozen peas, mixed 250g (9oz)
Plain flour 1 tbsp
Crème fraiche 200ml tub
Chopped parsley 3 tbsp, plus extra for sprinkling (optional)

Capers 2 tbsp
Salmon fillet 500g (1lb 2oz), skinned and cut into thumb-size chunks
Salt and freshly ground black pepper
Filo pastry 9 sheets (about 50g/2oz)
Sesame seeds 2 tsp

Preheat the oven to 200°C/400°F/Gas 6.

Put a quarter of the butter in a medium-sized mixing bowl with the leek. Microwave, covered, on 'high' for 2 minutes. Then add the sweetcorn and peas and microwave, covered, on 'high' for a further 2 minutes.

Mix the flour into the crème fraîche and then add the parsley and capers. Spread the mixture together with the vegetables into a fairly wide, shallow baking dish (about 1.5 litre /2½ pints capacity). Add the chunks of salmon to the baking dish and season well.

Add the rest of the butter to the mixing bowl and melt it in the microwave. Take one sheet of pastry at a time and brush it with butter, layering five buttered sheets on top of the filling.

Brush the rest of the sheets and arrange them on top, concertina-fashion, to cover the flat sheets. You may have to cut a few to fit and tuck ends underneath. Brush the top with any remaining butter and sprinkle with sesame seeds.

Bake for 25 minutes until the pastry is crisp and golden. Leave a few minutes then serve warm, sprinkled with extra parsley if you like.

COOK'S TIP
If you have filo pastry left over, the rest of the pack can be frozen or bake some other goodies, as suggested on the packaging.

105

Preparation time	**15 minutes**
Cooking time	**40 minutes**
Calories per portion	**937 Kcal**
Fat per portion	**59g**
of which saturated	**27.5g**
Serves	**4**

Chicken & ham pie

A deliciously creamy filling with a golden puff pastry top.

Cooked skinless, boneless chicken breasts 4, cubed
Ham, thickly sliced 150g (5oz), chopped
Button mushrooms 250g (9oz), wiped and quartered
Sweetcorn with peppers 198g can, drained
Cream cheese with herbs 125–150g tub
Stock cube 1, ham or chicken
Boiling water 4 tbsp
Double cream 150ml (¼ pint)
Salt and freshly ground black pepper
Puff pastry 375g packet, thawed if frozen
Egg 1, beaten

Preheat the oven to 220°C/425°F/Gas 7. Place the chicken, ham, mushrooms and sweetcorn in the base of a pie dish (about 1.25 litres/2 pint) capacity), and stir them to mix. Crumble over the cream cheese with herbs.

Dissolve the stock cube in the boiling water and then stir in the cream and seasoning. Pour this mixture into the pie dish.

Roll out the pastry on a lightly floured surface until it is just larger than the pie dish. Cut off around the edges of the pastry to give a 1cm (½in strip), brush water over the rim of the dish and then stick the strip of pastry on it. Brush water over the pastry rim and then lift the large piece of pastry over the top. Press it well around the edges to secure it in place.

Trim around the dish with a sharp knife to remove any excess. Use a sharp knife to make lots of cuts around the pastry edge to help the pastry rise. If liked, score a pattern on the top of the pie using the tip of a knife. Make one or two holes in the pastry in the centre of the pie to allow steam to escape.

Brush the beaten egg over the top of the pie. Bake in the centre of the oven for 30–40 minutes, or until the pastry is golden in colour and the filling is bubbling hot. Remove the pie from the oven and serve immediately with a Dressed leaves salad (see page 7).

COOK'S TIP
The cream cheese can be either cow's milk or goats' milk cheese; for example, try soft goats' cheese with chives and garlic.

Preparation time	10 minutes
Cooking time	1¾ hours
Calories per portion	951 Kcal
Fat per portion	64g
of which saturated	33.8g
Serves	4
Suitable for freezing	

Gruyère, bacon & potato gratin

Crumbly potatoes with smoky bacon and fragrant thyme.

Potatoes 1.5kg (3lb 4oz), such as Maris Piper, peeled and sliced
Onion 1, peeled and sliced
Smoked streaky bacon 12 rashers, chopped
Chopped thyme 2 tbsp or 1 tbsp dried
Stock cube 1, ham or vegetable
Boiling water 150ml (¼ pint)
Double cream 300ml (½ pint)
Milk 150ml (¼ pint)
Salt and freshly ground black pepper
Gruyère cheese 110g (4oz), grated

COOK'S TIP
This recipe can easily be converted to be a vegetarian recipe if the bacon is left out and a vegetable stock cube is used.

Preheat the oven to 180°C/350°F/Gas 4.

Layer up the potatoes, onion, bacon and thyme in a 2 litre (3½ pint) baking dish. Dissolve the stock cube in the boiling water and then stir in the cream and milk and season it well. Pour the mixture over the vegetables in the baking dish.

Cover the baking dish with a foil and place in the centre of the oven for 1 hour. Remove the foil and sprinkle with the cheese.

Return the dish to the oven with the foil back on and continue cooking the gratin for a further 30–45 minutes, removing the foil after 20 minutes for the gratin to turn a golden colour and the potatoes to feel tender when pierced with a knife. Remove from the oven and serve with a Bean salad (see page 7).

107

Preparation time	**10 minutes**
Cooking time	**40–50 minutes**
Calories per portion	**519 Kcal**
Fat per portion	**20g**
of which saturated	**10.6g**
Serves	**6**
Suitable for vegetarians	

Chocolate sauce pudding

An intense chocolate sauce with a fluffy sponge topping.

Self-raising flour 175g (6oz), sifted
Cocoa powder 85g (3½oz)
Butter 85g (3½oz)
Golden caster sugar 175g (6oz)
Full fat milk 200ml (7fl oz)
Golden caster sugar 125g (4½oz)
Cocoa powder 25g (1oz)
Boiling water 600ml (1 pint)

Preheat the oven to 170°C/325°F/Gas 3.

Sift the flour and cocoa powder into a bowl and rub in the butter. Stir in the sugar and mix in the milk until smooth (the mix will be quite stiff but it's meant to be). Spoon into a 1.75 litre (3 pint) ovenproof baking dish and level the surface.

Mix together the sugar and cocoa and whisk in the boiling water. Although this sounds odd, pour the cocoa liquid over the pudding and bake for 40–50 minutes or until the top is firm and there is a lovely dark sauce at the bottom.

Leave to stand for a minute or two only before serving – the sauce will be absorbed by the fluffy sponge if left to stand for too long.

COOK'S TIP
The exact cooking time depends on the depth of the dish you are using.

Preparation time	**20 minutes**
Cooking time	**1½ hours**
Calories per portion	**212 Kcal**
Fat per portion	**9g**
of which saturated	**5.8g**
Serves	**6**
Suitable for vegetarians	

Rich & fruity rice pudding

Comforting rice pudding with spice and fruit.

Butter 25g (1oz)
Pudding rice 75g (3oz)
Soft light brown sugar 25g (1oz)
Whole milk 900ml (1½ pints)
Ready-to-eat prunes 50g (2oz), roughly chopped
Ready-to-eat dried apricots 50g (2oz), roughly chopped
Vanilla bean 1, snipped along one side to release the vanilla curd
Ground cinnamon ½ tsp

Preheat the oven to 160°C/325°F/Gas 3. Lightly grease a 1.25 litre (2 pint) baking dish with a small amount of the butter.

Put the rice into a sieve, rinse under a cold running tap, and then shake off the excess water. Put the rice into the baking dish, and then add the sugar, milk, prunes and apricots – stir.

Add the vanilla bean and lightly sift the cinnamon over the top of the milk. Dot the top of the milk with small pieces of the remaining butter.

Cook the pudding in the centre of the oven for approximately 1½ hours, until the rice is softened and almost all of the milk has been absorbed – taking care not to over bake as the rice pudding will become dry. Serve hot.

COOK'S TIP
For a more traditional rice pudding, omit the dried fruits and add 1 teaspoon vanilla essence to the milk, rice and sugar. Sprinkle over a little grated nutmeg and dot with butter.

Preparation time	15 minutes
Cooking time	30 minutes
Calories per portion	388 Kcal
Fat per portion	25g
of which saturated	10.2g
Serves	6
Suitable for vegetarians	

Blueberry crumble

Blueberries given a sharp lemony edge beneath a comforting topping.

Blueberries 450g (1lb)
Caster sugar 150g (5oz)
Lemon 1, grated rind and juice
Breadcrumbs 75g (3oz)
Ground almonds 75g (3oz)
Butter 110g (4oz)
Slivered or flaked almonds 25g (1oz)

Preheat the oven to 200°C/400°F/Gas 6. Mix the fruit, 75g (3oz) of the sugar and lemon rind and juice in a shallow baking dish.

Make the crumble by mixing the breadcrumbs, ground almonds and remaining sugar in a large bowl. Rub in, or cut in, the butter roughly and spoon the mixture evenly over the fruit. Scatter with slivered or flaked almonds.

Bake the crumble for about 30 minutes, turning the oven heat down to 180°C/350°F/Gas 4 after 15 minutes when the top has browned. Serve warm or cold with plenty of cream – clotted or double!

COOK'S TIP
Crumbles are pretty flexible with the cooking temperature. If you're cooking other things in the oven at the same time, the crumble will cope – just cook it until it looks good.

Preparation time	15 minutes
Cooking time	30–40 minutes
Calories per portion	206 Kcal
Fat per portion	10.3g
of which saturated	3.5g
Serves	6
Suitable for vegetarians	

Bratapfel

Traditional German baked apples stuffed with almonds, ginger and marmalade.

Red dessert apples 6 medium–large
Almonds 40g (1½oz), lightly toasted and chopped
Stem ginger 25g (1oz), finely chopped
Marmalade 75g (3oz)
Unsalted butter 40g (1½oz)
Bay leaves to decorate
Icing sugar for sifting
Whipped cream or crème fraîche

Preheat the oven to 220°C/425°F/ Gas 7. With an apple corer, make a hole in the centre of each apple, approximately 2.5cm (1in) wide. Place the apples in a shallow baking dish.

Mix together the almonds, ginger and marmalade and spoon into each apple – pressing down well. Dot the tops of the apples with butter.

Add 2 tablespoons of water to the baking dish and cook in the oven for 30–40 minutes, until the apples are golden and softened. Baste occasionally with the juices.

Serve the apples on individual plates, drizzled with juices and decorated with bay leaves lightly sifted with icing sugar. Accompany with whipped cream or crème fraîche.

COOK'S TIP
If you're not fond of ginger, replace it with an equal quantity of dried fruits, finely chopped.

Preparation time	**15 minutes**
Cooking time	**1 hour 15 minutes**
Calories per square	**228 Kcal**
Fat per square	**9.8g**
of which saturated	**5.6g**
Makes	**16 squares**
Suitable for freezing	
Suitable for vegetarians	

Cherry bread pudding

Moist and sticky with glistening succulent fruit.

White bread 2–3 days old, crust removed: 225g (8oz), bread torn into small pieces
Milk 375ml (13fl oz)
Oranges 2, grated rind of both, juice of 1
Mixed ground spice 1 tbsp
Seedless raisins 175g (6oz)
Sultanas 150g (5oz)
Mixed chopped peel 50g (2oz)
Ready-to-eat prunes 75g (3oz), chopped
Ready-to-eat dried apricots 75g (3oz), chopped
Glacé cherries 75g (3oz), quartered
Eggs 3, beaten
Butter 150g (5oz), melted
Black treacle 1–2 tbsp
Granulated sugar

COOK'S TIP
If serving warm with custard, stir a little extra grated orange rind and a tablespoon or two of sherry into the custard when reheating.

Preheat the oven to 180°C/350°F/Gas 4 and grease a 23cm (9in) square shallow baking dish.

Soak the bread with the milk in a bowl for 10 minutes. Add the rest of the ingredients, except the sugar, and mix well. Transfer to the baking dish, spread evenly and bake for 45–50 minutes until the pudding is lightly browned and set in the centre.

Sprinkle with the granulated sugar and serve hot with custard. Or leave to cool, cut into squares, cover and refrigerate.

Baking sheet

What could be more pleasingly simple than a baking sheet? It's a basic device for spreading heat under a dish and letting it cook on its own.

The classic use for a baking sheet is to support pizza – and here we have a wonderful variation on the standard theme with the Onion, mushroom & goats' cheese pizza. Using food as a container is another long-known technique and in this chapter we have examples such as Chinese-style Baked stuffed peppers, rich, buttery Cornish pasties and the pâté-in-pastry Pork Wellington. Desserts include a rainbow of fruits stuffed into dumplings while puff pastry features in the Blueberry & apple bake.

Preparation time **10 minutes**

Cooking time **10–12 minutes**

Calories per portion **406 Kcal**

Fat per portion **16g**

of which saturated **10.3g**

Serves **2**

Suitable for vegetarians

Onion, mushroom & goats' cheese pizza

Tangy goats' cheese contrasting with velvety mushrooms.

Thin and crispy pizza base 1
Organic onion relish 2–3 tbsp
Tomatoes 2, thinly sliced
Baby mushrooms 50g (2oz), wiped and sliced
Goats' cheese 110g (4oz), sliced and broken into chunks
Green pesto sauce about 1 tbsp (optional)
Salt and freshly ground black pepper
Wild rocket about 15g (½oz)

Preheat the oven to 220ºC/425ºF/Gas 7.

Put the pizza base onto a baking sheet. Spread the onion relish on the top to make a thin layer. Scatter the tomatoes and mushrooms on top. Add the goats' cheese and bake for 10–12 minutes or until the pizza is golden and cooked.

Quickly spread green pesto sauce over the top of the pizza, if using. Season to taste and serve with a handful of rocket in the centre.

COOK'S TIP
Don't go mad with the onion relish – it is strong and quite sweet but cuts through the richness of the goats' cheese beautifully.

Preparation time	**5 minutes**
Cooking time	**30 minutes**
Calories per portion	**350 Kcal**
Fat per portion	**17g**
of which saturated	**3.7g**
Serves	**4**
Suitable for vegetarians	

Baked stuffed peppers

A Chinese-style tasty rice stuffing in soft and sweet peppers.

Red peppers 4 large, halved and deseeded
Olive oil 1 tbsp
Egg-fried rice 250g carton
Sweetcorn 198g can, drained
Frozen peas 50g (2oz)
Chopped coriander 1 tbsp
Salt and freshly ground black pepper
Eggs 8 medium

Preheat the oven to 200°C/400°F/ Gas 6.

Place the peppers on a baking sheet and brush them on the inside and cut edges with the olive oil. Place the baking sheet in the oven and bake the peppers for 15 minutes.

Meanwhile, mix together the egg-fried rice, sweetcorn, peas, coriander and seasoning.

Remove the peppers from the oven and spoon the rice mixture into the cavities, pressing the mixture down well and hollowing it slightly in the centre. Break an egg into each pepper and grind a little black pepper on top of each one.

Return the baking sheet with the peppers to the oven and bake for a further 12–15 minutes, or until the eggs have just set.

Remove the peppers from the oven and serve two halves per person, with soy sauce to drizzle over the rice. Accompany with Creamy dressed leaves salad (see page 7) if you like.

COOK'S TIP
When cutting the peppers in half, cut through the stalks as the peppers look more stylish with the stalks left on them.

Preparation time	5 minutes
Cooking time	25 minutes
Calories per portion	348 Kcal
Fat per portion	18g
of which saturated	3.4g
Serves	4

Crispy chicken

Golden breadcrumbed chicken breasts served with cherry tomatoes on the vine.

Mayonnaise 3 tbsp
Sun-dried tomato purée 1 tbsp
Fresh white breadcrumbs 4 tbsp
Grated Parmesan cheese 2 tbsp
Skinless, boneless chicken breasts 4
Freshly ground black pepper
Olive oil 2 tbsp
Cherry tomatoes on the vine 300g (11oz)

COOK'S TIP
It's easy to put together an Italian-style salad. Mix rocket, basil and radicchio leaves and lightly chopped plum tomatoes. Drizzle with balsamic vinegar and a little olive oil.

Preheat the oven to 200°C/400°F/Gas 6. In a bowl, mix together the mayonnaise and tomato purée, and in another bowl mix together the breadcrumbs and cheese. Set aside. Wash and pat dry the chicken breasts with kitchen paper. Place on a baking sheet lined with baking parchment. Season with black pepper.

Spread the chicken breasts thickly with 1 tablespoon of the tomato mayonnaise. Then pat on the breadcrumb mixture, making sure the chicken is well coated.

Drizzle each breast with olive oil and then bake in the oven for 20–25 minutes until golden, tender and cooked through. Add the cherry tomatoes on the vine for the last 10 minutes of chicken cooking time. Serve hot accompanied with the remaining mayonnaise.

Preparation time	10 minutes
Cooking time	1 hour 10 minutes
Calories per portion	585 Kcal
Fat per portion	34g
of which saturated	13g
Serves	4

Pork Wellington

Tender pork and mushroom pâté wrapped in a light golden pastry.

Ready-rolled puff pastry 375g packet
Mushroom or Ardennes pâté 115g carton
Rocket leaves 25g (1oz)
Marinated and grilled red and yellow peppers 200g pack
Salt and freshly ground black pepper
Pork tenderloin 450g (1lb)
Egg 1, beaten

Preheat the oven to 220°C/425°F/ Gas 7. Line a large baking sheet with baking parchment.

Unroll the puff pastry and trim around the edges of it. Spread the pâté over the pastry, leaving a clear border of 2cm (¾in) all around the edges. Top with half the rocket and peppers. Add seasoning, lay the pork on top and then add the remaining rocket and peppers.

Brush around the clear edges of the pastry with water. Wrap the pastry lengthways around the pork and then press the join well where the pastry overlaps. Place the seam underneath and fold under each end to seal the pastry parcel. Place the pastry on the lined baking tray.

Use the tip of a sharp knife to score the pastry to make a pattern, but don't cut all the way through it. Make one or two small holes completely through the pastry to allow steam to escape. Brush the beaten egg over the pastry.

Bake the pastry parcel in the centre of the oven for 10 minutes, then reduce the temperature to 180°C/350°C/ Gas 4 and cook for a further 45 minutes–1 hour, or until the juices run clear when a fine skewer is pressed through the side of the pastry into the meat. The pork Wellington may be served hot or warm, with a creamy Dressed leaves salad (see page 7).

COOK'S TIP
If you don't have a baking tray that is large enough to take the whole length of the pastry, cut the pork into four pieces and make individual parcels.

Preparation time	30 minutes
Cooking time	25 minutes
Calories per pastie	630 Kcal
Fat per pastie	35g
of which saturated	16.8g
Makes	4 pasties

Suitable for freezing

Cornish pasties

Rich buttery pastry encases a tender and tasty filling of meat and vegetables.

Potato 1, peeled and very finely diced
Carrot 1, peeled and very finely diced
Small onion 1, peeled and very finely diced
Lean beef steak 225g (8oz), trimmed and cut into small pieces
Salt and freshly ground black pepper
Shortcrust pastry 450g (1lb)
Egg 1, beaten

Preheat the oven to 220°C/425°F/Gas 7. Mix together the potato, carrot, onion and steak and season well.

Roll out the pastry thinly on a lightly floured surface. Cut three saucer-sized circles, then use the trimmings to make a fourth. Divide the meat and vegetables between each circle, and brush the edges with egg.

Bring up the edges of each pasty circle to meet at the top. Crimp together the edges by pinching gently with the finger and thumb to seal.

Place on a baking sheet and brush all over with beaten egg. Bake for 10 minutes, then reduce the heat to 180°C/350°F/Gas 4 and cook for a further 15–20 minutes until golden and cooked through. Allow to cool for 10 minutes before serving with cherry tomatoes and a Bean salad (see page 7).

COOK'S TIP
To freeze, allow to cool and then open freeze on trays or boards. Pack in a freezer bag or freezer-proof container and return to the freezer for up to three months.

Preparation time	45–50 minutes
Cooking time	30–40 minutes
Calories per dumpling	919 Kcal
Fat per dumpling	46g
of which saturated	23.9g
Makes	4 dumplings

Suitable for vegetarians

Apple dumplings

Plump apples stuffed with dried fruits encased in crisp pastry.

Plain flour 350g (12oz)
Caster sugar 40g (1½oz)
Butter 175g (6oz)
Egg 1 large, beaten
Soft light brown or caster sugar 25g (1oz)
Ground almonds 50g (2oz)
Dark glacé cherries 25g (1oz), cut small
Ready-to-eat prunes 25g (1oz), cut small

Ready-to-eat dried apricots 25g (1oz), cut small
Clear honey 1 tbsp
Cooking apples 4, approximately 225g (8oz) each
Milk for basting
Caster sugar 1 tbsp
Icing sugar 1 tbsp

To make the pastry, sift the flour into a mixing bowl, add the caster sugar and rub in the butter until the mixture resembles fine breadcrumbs. Add the beaten egg and 2–3 tablespoons cold water and mix to form a soft, but not sticky, dough. Wrap with cling film and chill in the fridge.

To prepare the filling, put the sugar, almonds, glacé cherries, prunes, apricots and honey into a small bowl and mix together well.

Preheat the oven to 200°C/400°F/Gas 6. Lightly grease a large baking sheet or line it with non-stick foil. Remove the apple cores with an apple corer or small pointed knife, making a hole approximately 2.5cm (1in) in diameter. Then peel the apples, place on a plate and fill the centres with the almond mixture, pressing it down firmly into the holes.

Roll out the pastry thinly, then use a 20cm (8in) plate as a guide to cut out four rounds from the pastry, re-kneading and rolling the trimmings as necessary. Make little leaves from pastry trimmings and drape over crumpled foil.

Place one of the apples top-side down in the centre of one of the pastry rounds, and then bring the pastry up and over the apple to enclose it completely – moulding it smoothly. Brush the joins lightly with water and then place the apple, join side down, on the prepared baking sheet. Using a small skewer, make a small hole in the top of each apple so the steam can escape as it cooks.

COOK'S TIP
If you are short of time, use a 500g (1lb 2oz) pack of shortcrust pastry, defrosted if frozen.

Brush the dumplings and leaves with milk, sprinkle them lightly with caster sugar and then bake for 35–45 minutes (removing the leaves after 10–15 minutes) until the pastry is cooked and lightly browned and the apples are softened (test by inserting a skewer through the side of the pastry). Transfer onto serving plates, add the leaves, sift lightly with icing sugar and serve immediately accompanied with scoops of vanilla ice cream.

Preparation time	15 minutes, plus chilling
Cooking time	18 minutes
Calories per biscuit	81 Kcal
Fat per biscuit	4.1g
of which saturated	2.5g
Makes	24 biscuits

Dough suitable for freezing

Suitable for vegetarians

Wild blueberry biscuits

Traditional biscuits with a twist – blueberries in place of currants.

Plain flour 175g (6oz)
Mixed spice 1 tsp
Butter 110g (4oz)
Caster sugar 110g (4oz), plus extra
for sprinkling
Lemon 1, grated zest
Wild blueberries 75g (3oz) (see
Cook's Tip)
Egg 1, beaten

Sift the flour and spice into a large
bowl. Add slivers of butter and then
rub it in with your fingertips. Stir in
the sugar, lemon zest and blueberries
and then add the egg and mix to a
firm dough.

Knead the dough briefly on a lightly
floured surface and shape into a
sausage about 20cm (8in) long and
about 5cm (2in) wide. Wrap in cling
film and chill in the fridge for an hour
or in the freezer for half an hour.

Preheat the oven to 180°C/350°F/
Gas 4 and lightly grease a large baking
sheet. Unwrap the chilled dough and
cut into 5mm (¼in) thick slices. Put
them on the baking sheet, spaced a
little apart.

Bake the biscuits for 15–18 minutes
until they are pale golden in colour.
Cool on the baking sheet for a few
minutes, sprinkle with a little caster
sugar and then transfer the biscuits to
a wire rack to cool.

COOK'S TIP
The wild blueberries in this recipe are semi-
dried and are available in tubs in the same
fixture in the supermarket as the dried fruits.

Preparation time	20 minutes
Cooking time	4 hours, plus
	30 minutes cooling
Calories per portion	363 Kcal
Fat per portion	20g
of which saturated	11.3g
Serves	8

Suitable for vegetarians

Meringue with summer fruits

Light, crisp sugary meringue topped with cream and ripe berries.

Eggs 5, whites only
Caster sugar 300g (11oz)
Double cream 300ml (½ pint)
Raspberries 350g (12oz)
Strawberries 350g (12oz) small, halved, retaining the hulls on some to decorate

Preheat the oven to 110ºC/225ºF/Gas ¼. Line a baking sheet with baking parchment and draw a 20cm (8in) circle in the centre.

Using an electric mixer, whisk the egg whites until stiff, then gradually whisk in the sugar until you have a thick, glossy meringue. Spoon one-third of the meringue into a circle within the drawn line on the paper and then, using a dessertspoon, spoon a border of meringue over the edge of the circle. Finish making the dessert with a second layer of spooned meringue around the top edge to make a basket.

Bake for about 4 hours or until the meringue is pale and crisp. Leave to cool for about half an hour, remove the parchment and leave to cool completely.

Whip the cream until thick, spoon onto the meringue and pile all the fruit on top, leaving the strawberries with hulls until last. Serve within 3 hours of assembly.

COOK'S TIP
Use any summer fruit that you have to hand, blueberries, stoned cherries, blackberries and loganberries work very well. Just ensure they total 700g (1lb 8oz).

Preparation time	20 minutes
Cooking time	25 minutes
Calories per portion	373 Kcal
Fat per portion	19.1g
of which saturated	6.6g
Serves	8

Suitable for freezing

Suitable for vegetarians

Blueberry & apple bake

A puff pastry parcel with almond flavouring and soft fruits.

Dessert apples 450g (1lb), peeled, cored and sliced
Caster sugar 75g (3oz)
Lemon 1, grated zest and juice
Blueberries 150g (5oz), stalks removed
Mixed ground spice 1½ tsp
Plain flour 1 tbsp
Puff pastry 500g packet, thawed if frozen
Ground almonds 50g (2oz)
Egg 1, beaten
Granulated sugar 1–2 tbsp
Honey for drizzling

Preheat the oven to 220°C/425°F/ Gas 7. In a large bowl, mix together the dessert apples, caster sugar, lemon zest and juice, blueberries, mixed ground spice and flour.

Roll the pastry into a 40cm (16in) square, trim the edges and cut in half. Place one strip on a baking tray. Spread the ground almonds down the centre and spoon the apple mixture on top. Fold the other strip in half lengthways and make cuts evenly along the fold to within 2.5cm (1in) of the cut edges.

Brush the pastry around the fruit with egg. Cover with the second strip, unfolding over the fruit. Press the edges together, brush with egg and sprinkle with granulated sugar.

Bake for 25 minutes until the pastry is golden brown and the apples softened. Drizzle honey through the slits and serve hot.

COOK'S TIP
The choice of filling can be varied. Try a mix of stoned and thickly sliced plums and pears, peaches and blueberries or strudel style with spiced apples and sultanas.

Preparation time	20 minutes
Cooking time	10 minutes
Calories per cake	295 Kcal
Fat per cake	16g
of which saturated	9.8g
Makes	12 cakes

Suitable for vegetarians

Suitable for freezing

Jammy cakes

Two cakey biscuits sandwiched together with raspberry jam.

Unsalted butter 225g (8oz), softened
Caster sugar 110g (4oz)
Self-raising flour 350g (12oz)
Salt ½ tsp
Raspberry jam 6 tbsp
Icing sugar 1 tbsp

COOK'S TIP
The cakes spread a little during cooking so don't place them too close together on the baking sheets – allow approximately 2.5cm (1in) between each one.

Preheat the oven to 180°C/350°F/Gas 4. In a bowl, mix together the butter and sugar until creamy and smooth, and gradually work in the flour and salt.

Bring together to form a firm dough and turn on to a lightly floured surface. Roll out to a thickness of 6mm (¼in) and, using a 5cm (2in) pastry cutter, cut out 24 rounds, re-rolling the dough as necessary. Cut holes from the middle of 12 rounds using a smaller cutter or the upturned end of a large piping nozzle.

Arrange slightly spaced apart on baking sheets lined with baking parchment and bake for about 10 minutes until risen and golden. Allow to cool on the baking sheets and then transfer to a cooling rack. Sandwich the rounds together with jam and dust lightly with icing sugar just before serving.

127

Roasting tin

You might think that a roasting tin has its limitations for one-pot cuisine, but this is far from the case.

A roasting tin can be used for so much more than a traditional roast: it can hold the deliciously cheesy pasta of a Squash & pepper pasta bake, and it will also retain the wonderful sauces created by the meat juices as in the honey, orange and soy sauce of our Spatchcock chicken. For a spicier take on white meat, try the Tandoori-style poussins with its yogurt marinade. Stuffed dishes roast well because of the different textures outside and in, as with the Black pudding-stuffed pork or the Baked marrow with mince. To finish, try the unusual combination of Slow-roast pears with orange & aniseed.

Preparation time	**10 minutes**
Cooking time	**20 minutes**
Calories per portion	**407 Kcal**
Fat per portion	**26g**
of which saturated	**6.5g**
Serves	**4**

Suitable for vegetarians

Nutty pesto tomatoes

Big juicy tomatoes with a crunchy pesto-infused filling.

Beef tomatoes 4
Ciabatta rolls 2
Green pesto sauce 180g jar
Salt and freshly ground black pepper
Olive oil 3 tbsp
Pine nuts 2 tbsp

Halve the tomatoes horizontally then carefully scoop the flesh into a large bowl. Place the tomato shells in a roasting tin.

Tear the ciabatta into pieces. Put into a food processor and whizz to coarse crumbs. Add the crumbs and pesto to the tomato flesh and mix thoroughly, seasoning to taste.

Spoon the tomato mixture into the shells, then drizzle with a little olive oil and a sprinkling of pine nuts.

Bake in the oven for 15–20 minutes, until the tomatoes are softened and the topping is golden. Serve immediately.

COOK'S TIP
This simple recipe is only as good as the tomatoes, so buy those that are still on the vine for the best flavour.

Preparation time	15 minutes
Cooking time	50 minutes
Calories per portion	662 Kcal
Fat per portion	34g
of which saturated	16.5g
Serves	4

Suitable for vegetarians

Squash & pepper pasta bake

Naturally sweet golden vegetables with penne pasta and cheese sauce.

Butternut squash 1, peeled, deseeded and cut into bite-size chunks

Onion 1, peeled, cut into 8 wedges and leaves pulled apart

Red pepper 1, quartered, deseeded and cut into big chunks

Yellow pepper 1, quartered, deseeded and cut into big chunks

Butter about 25g (1oz)

Olive oil 1 tbsp

Salt and freshly ground black pepper

Fresh penne 250g pack

Ready-made four-cheese sauce 350g tub

Spinach leaves 110g (4oz), roughly chopped

Tomatoes 4, sliced

Cheddar cheese 110g (4oz), coarsely grated

Preheat the oven to 200°C/400°F/Gas 6. Put a non-stick roasting tin in the oven to heat up while you prepare the squash, onion and peppers.

Add the butter and oil to the tin and then toss in the squash and onion and coat well. Roast for 15 minutes, then stir in the pepper pieces and seasoning and cook for another 15 minutes.

Five minutes after adding the pepper to the tin, put the pasta into a large mixing bowl and pour over enough boiling water to cover it. Stir and leave for 5 minutes.

Microwave the sauce in its pot, according to the pack's instructions until hot.

Drain the pasta, put it back in the bowl, then stir in the spinach and let it wilt. Stir in the hot cheese sauce. Spread this mixture over the vegetables in the tin. Arrange the sliced tomatoes on top and sprinkle with the grated cheese.

Return to the oven and bake for 25 minutes until browned and piping hot. Leave to stand for 5 minutes then serve with a Refreshing salsa (see page 7).

COOK'S TIP
Cut the squash into thick slices (about 1cm/½in) and then each slice into six wedges so they are an even size.

131

Preparation time	10 minutes
Cooking time	25 minutes
Calories per portion	610 Kcal
Fat per portion	40g
of which saturated	11.5g
Serves	2

Summer roast salmon

Roast salmon fillets served with a piquant creamy dip.

New potatoes 6–8, scrubbed and cut into half lengthways
Olive oil 2 tbsp
Salmon fillets 2, about 150g (5oz) each
Asparagus spears 10–12 spears, trimmed
Small tomatoes on the vine 10–12
Lemon ½, grated zest and juice
Chopped parsley and/or tarragon 1 tbsp
Capers 1 tbsp, chopped if large
Black olives 4, pitted and chopped
Crème fraîche 2 heaped tbsp

Preheat the oven to 200°C/400°F/Gas 6. Put a large, heavy, shallow roasting tin into the oven to heat up while you prepare the potatoes. Spoon in half of the oil and toss in the potatoes to coat them and spread them out, cut side down, in one layer in the tin. Roast for 15 minutes.

After 15 minutes, turn the potatoes and push them to one side of the tin. Add the fish fillets, the asparagus spears and tomatoes. Sprinkle them with the rest of the oil and squeeze a little lemon juice over the fish. Bake for 10 minutes.

To make the sauce, mix most of the lemon zest and remaining lemon juice and chopped herbs (reserving some for garnish), along with the capers and black olives, into the crème fraîche.

Serve the fish on warmed plates on a bed of vegetables with more lemon juice squeezed over the top and the remaining zest and chopped parsley/tarragon scattered over. Place a dollop of the dipping sauce alongside.

COOK'S TIP
To ensure even cooking, have all the potatoes the same size and the asparagus spears the same width, and choose the thickest fillets of fish that you can buy.

Preparation time	15 minutes
Cooking time	30 minutes
Calories per portion	411 Kcal
Fat per portion	10g
of which saturated	1.8g
Serves	2

Fish & chips

Golden chunky chips with succulent cod and tartare sauce.

Potatoes 500g (1lb 2oz), peeled and cut into chunky chips
Olive oil 1 tbsp
Plain flour 2 tsp
Salt and freshly ground black pepper
Chopped dill 2 tbsp
Skinless, boneless cod fillets 2, weighing about 150g (5oz) each
Egg 1, beaten
Lemon wedges
Tartare sauce

Preheat the oven to 220ºC/425ºF/ Gas 7. Cook the chips on high for 3 minutes in the microwave. Toss the chips in 2 tsp of the oil

Arrange the chips in a single layer at one end of a large non-stick roasting tin and cook for about 30 minutes, or until the chips are tender and golden.

Meanwhile, mix together the flour, seasoning and dill on a plate, toss the cod fillets in the seasoned flour, then the beaten egg and back in to the flour mix. Remove the roasting tin from the oven and, using a fish slice, carefully turn the chips. Drizzle the remaining oil at the other end of the tin. Add the cod to the oiled roasting tin and continue to cook for the last 10–15 minutes of the chips' cooking time, or until the cod is tender.

Serve the cod and chips with lemon wedges, tartare sauce and a Fruit and nuts salad (see page 7).

COOK'S TIP
Instead of peeling the potatoes to make the chips, wash the potatoes and leave the skin on before cutting into wedges.

Preparation time	30 minutes
Cooking time	1 hour 10 minutes
Calories per portion	431 Kcal
Fat per portion	27g
of which saturated	7.9g
Serves	4

Spatchcock chicken

Roasted chicken cooked in honey, orange and soy sauce.

Chicken approximately 1.65–1.8kg
(3½–4lb)
**Salt and freshly ground black
pepper**
Oranges 2 large
Clear honey 3 tbsp
Sun-dried tomato paste 2 tbsp
Light soy sauce 2 tbsp

COOK'S TIP
The chicken may be prepared up to the pouring of the orange juice mixture over it and be kept, covered, in the refrigerator until ready to cook. Allow a little extra cooking time.

Preheat the oven to 220°C/425°F/Gas 7. Rinse the chicken well under a cold running tap, and then dry thoroughly with kitchen paper towel.

Place the chicken, breast side down, on a chopping board and then, using poultry shears or a large sharp knife, remove the backbone, by cutting down each side. If using a knife, take extra care to ensure the knife does not slip (for added safety, place a clean, folded tea towel over the knife, and then, holding the knife firmly, tap the back of the knife with a heavy kitchen weight).

Place the chicken breast-side up on the board and open it out flat. Make a small cut in the skin between the tip of the breastbone and each leg. Then insert the top of each leg bone into the slits to keep the legs and thighs firmly in place. Lay the chicken in a roasting tin, skin-side up, and then season well.

Cut the oranges into quarters and squeeze out the juice from four of them. Put the orange juice, honey, sun-dried tomato paste and soy sauce into a bowl, whisk well together and then pour over the chicken. Place the remaining orange quarters in the roasting tin.

Roast the chicken for 30–40 minutes, then reduce the heat to 180°C/350°F/Gas 4 and, if necessary, cover with foil to stop the chicken from over browning. Continue to cook for another 30–45 minutes, or until the chicken is cooked, basting frequently. When cooked, remove the chicken from the roasting tin onto a serving plate and keep warm.

Using a tablespoon, skim off all the fat from the top of the roasting juices. Reheat the juices in the oven if necessary and then strain them through a sieve into a small jug. Serve the juices with the chicken and accompanied with a Bean salad (see page 7) and warm Mediterranean-style bread.

Preparation time	**45 minutes, plus**
	1–3 hours marinating
Cooking time	**45 minutes–1 hour**
Calories per portion	**797 Kcal**
Fat per portion	**43g**
of which saturated	**12.9g**
Serves	**4**

Tandoori-style poussins

Poussins marinaded in spicy yogurt served with warm naan bread.

Lemons 2 large, grated zest and juice
Sea salt 1 tsp
Saffron threads ½ tsp, soaked in
2 tbsp boiling water
Poussins 4 x 450g (1lb)

For the marinade
Natural yogurt 275g (10oz)
Root ginger 7.5cm (3in) piece, peeled
and finely grated
Curry powder, medium hot 3–4 tsp
Garlic 2 large cloves, peeled and
crushed
Onion 1 large, peeled and finely
chopped
Red food colouring 1 tsp
Lemon 1, grated zest only

Naan bread 2–3, heated as instructed
on the packet

COOK'S TIP
The yogurt mixture forms a soft,
but firm coating over the poussins,
which adds a delicious flavour, and
keeps them moist and very tender.

Rinse the insides of the poussins under a cold running tap, then dry thoroughly
with kitchen paper. Using a sharp knife, make two long, deep cuts in each side
of the breasts, and two in each leg.

Put the lemon zest and juice, salt and saffron threads into a large bowl, stir
until the salt dissolves. Add the poussins and spoon the mixture over each one –
and especially into the cuts. Cover and set aside while making the marinade.

Mix together all the ingredients for the marinade in a jug, pour it over the
poussins and then turn them gently until they are evenly coated. Cover the bowl
and refrigerate for 1–3 hours, or overnight, if preferred.

To cook, preheat the oven to 200°C/400°F/Gas 6. Line a large roasting tin with
foil (makes cleaning easier) and then place a lightly oiled roasting rack (or wire
rack) in the bottom of the tin.

Remove the poussins from the marinade (without removing their yogurt
coating), place them on the wire rack and cook in the centre of the oven for
50–60 minutes, or until their juices run clear. Test with the tip of a knife inserted
into the thickest part of the thighs and the inside of the leg.

Just before the poussins are ready, put the naan breads in the oven to heat
through. Serve the poussins accompanied with the naan bread.

Preparation time	15 minutes
Cooking time	45 minutes
Calories per portion	510 Kcal
Fat per portion	35.5g
of which saturated	17.4g
Serves	4

Cheese-stuffed chops

Pork chops stuffed with herby cheese and horseradish in a rich creamy sauce.

Red Leicester cheese 50g (2oz), grated
Low fat soft cheese 75g (3oz)
Fresh breadcrumbs 25g (1oz)
Horseradish sauce 1 tbsp
Chopped parsley 2 tsp
Pork chops 4 x 150g (5oz)
Butter 25g (1oz)
Parsnips 3, peeled and cut into thin wedges
Onions 2, peeled, halved and cut into wedges
Olive oil 1 tbsp
Sherry 3 tbsp
Double cream 3 tbsp

Preheat the oven to 190°C/375°F/ Gas 5. In a bowl, mix together the cheeses, breadcrumbs, horseradish and parsley. Cut a deep pocket in the flesh of each chop and fill with the cheese mixture.

Melt the butter in a roasting tin. Add the chops and fry to brown on both sides. Then add the parsnips and onion wedges and drizzle with the olive oil. Cover the chops with foil and bake in the oven for 20 minutes. Uncover and cook for a further 20 minutes.

Remove the tin from the oven, take out the chops and vegetables and keep them warm. Add the sherry to the tin, scrape up any sediment and mix in well. Bring to the boil on the hob and cook until reduced to a syrup. Remove from the heat and stir in the cream. Spoon the creamy sauce over the chops and serve with the roasted vegetables.

COOK'S TIP
Sour cream in place of the double cream is just as good, but with a slightly tarter taste.

Preparation time	**10 minutes**
Cooking time	**30–35 minutes**
Calories per portion	**261 Kcal**
Fat per portion	**18g**
of which saturated	**9.1g**
Serves	**4**

Roast vegetables with bacon

Buttery winter vegetables oven-roasted with crisp bacon.

Butter 50g (2oz)
Parsnips 2, peeled and each cut into 6 wedges
Leeks 2, trimmed and cut in half and then in half again lengthways
Celery 2 large sticks, cut in half and then in half again lengthways
Dessert apple 1, quartered, cored and each piece cut into 3 wedges
Unsmoked back bacon 8 rashers
Baby spinach 4 good handfuls
Salt and freshly ground black pepper

Preheat the oven to 220°C/425°F/Gas 7 and put a large roasting tin in the oven to heat up.

Add the butter to the hot roasting tin and when it melts, put all the vegetables and apple wedges into the tin and turn them to coat in the butter. They should all fit in one layer. Roast for 10 minutes.

Lay the rashers of bacon on top and roast for a further 20 minutes. Turn over the bacon and vegetables and cook for another 5–10 minutes until the bacon is crispy and the vegetables tender and browning.

To serve, put a handful of spinach leaves on each plate. Arrange the roasted vegetables, apple and bacon on top and spoon over the buttery cooking juices. Season to taste and serve immediately.

COOK'S TIP
Use good quality dry cured bacon so that it cooks and browns evenly. With cheaper bacon you may get white watery juices oozing out, which doesn't look good.

Preparation time	**15 minutes**
Cooking time	**25 minutes**
Calories per portion	**354 Kcal**
Fat per portion	**24g**
of which saturated	**6.3g**
Serves	**4**

Black pudding-stuffed pork

The rich distinctive taste of black pudding in bacon-wrapped pork parcels.

Pork escalopes 4 thin, approximately 350g (12oz) total weight
Salt and freshly ground black pepper
Black pudding 200g (7oz)
Smoked streaky bacon 4 rashers
Butter 25g (1oz), melted

Preheat the oven to 200°C/400°F/ Gas 6. Butter a small roasting tin.

Lay the pork on the worksurface and season it. Remove any skin from the black pudding and divide it into four. Shape the black pudding into sausage shapes, just shorter than the width of the escalopes. Place a sausage of black pudding on each escalope and roll the pork around it.

Use the back of a knife to stretch the bacon and then wrap one rasher around each rolled-up escalope. Place each escalope on the buttered roasting tin and brush the melted butter over the escalopes.

Bake the escalopes in the oven for 20–30 minutes, or until the bacon has crisped, and the pork juices run clear when pierced with a fine skewer.

Serve the pork escalopes either whole or slice them and arrange them on plates. Serve with a Creamy dressed leaves salad (see page 7).

COOK'S TIP
If you are unable to find thin escalopes, then use four pieces of pork tenderloin. Place each piece in a plastic bag and beat it out with a rolling pin until it is thin.

Preparation time	30 minutes
Cooking time	2 hours
Calories per portion	854 Kcal
Fat per portion	44g
of which saturated	16.3g
Serves	6

Sweet 'n' sour pork loin roast

Roast pork with a twist: cooked in a subtle sweet and sour sauce.

Pork loin roast on the bone, skin removed 2.7kg (6lb) prepared weight
Spring onions 4–6, trimmed
Coarsely ground black peppercorns 1–2 tsp
Salt
Potatoes 500g (1lb 2oz), peeled and cut into wedges
Carrots 3 large, peeled and cut into chunks
Red onions 2 large, cut into quarters (skins left on)
Sweet potatoes 350g (12oz)

For the basting sauce
Olive oil 1 tbsp
Ground ginger 1 tsp
Teriyaki sauce 3 tbsp
Soy sauce 1 tbsp
Clear honey 3 tbsp
Rice vinegar or white vinegar 3 tbsp
Chicken stock 225ml (8fl oz)
Tomato paste 1 rounded tbsp

COOK'S TIP
You can ask your butcher to remove the pork's skin, if you wish. Any leftover pork can be eaten cold with salad.

Preheat the oven to 230°C/450°F/Gas 8.

Wipe the pork thoroughly with white kitchen paper. Then, using a long carving knife, insert it right the way through the centre of the meat – if necessary, insert the knife through the meat from both ends.

Season the spring onions well with the coarsely ground black pepper and insert them, from both ends, into the cut in the meat. Using a small sharp knife, lightly score the fat of the meat in a diamond pattern and then season it with salt.

Place the loin (fat-side up, bones down) in a large roasting tin and roast in the oven for 1 hour, basting frequently with the pork's own fat and juices.

Remove the roasting tin from the oven, add all the prepared vegetables and turn them in the pork juices until they are evenly coated. Return to the oven and continue cooking for 25–30 minutes, until slightly softened. Meanwhile, mix together the ingredients for the basting sauce.

Remove the roasting tin from the oven once more, spoon off excess fat and pour the basting sauce evenly over the meat and vegetables and then return to the oven and cook for a further 25–30 minutes, or until the vegetables and the meat are cooked through, basting frequently. Serve immediately.

Preparation time	**10 minutes**
Cooking time	**30 minutes**
Calories per portion	**512 Kcal**
Fat per portion	**34g**
of which saturated	**10g**
Serves	**4**

Sausages baked with apples & squash

Autumnal squash and spiced apple baked with sausage and maple syrup.

Butternut squash or pumpkin 1 small
Red onion 1, peeled and thickly sliced
Granny Smith apples 2, cored, peeled and thickly sliced
Lemon juice 2 tbsp
Maple syrup 2 tbsp
Ground cinnamon 1 tsp
Vegetable oil 2 tbsp
Salt and freshly ground black pepper
Thick pork sausages 8
Chopped parsley 2 tbsp

Preheat the oven to 200°C/400°F/ Gas 6. Line a medium-sized roasting tin with baking parchment.

Cut the squash or pumpkin in half and scoop out the seeds. Slice off the skin and then cut into wedges about 2cm (¾in) thick. Arrange evenly in the tin with the onion and apple slices.

In a small bowl, mix together the lemon juice, maple syrup, cinnamon and oil, and drizzle over the vegetables, carefully mixing them on the tray to coat them in the mixture. Season well.

Arrange the sausages on top and bake with the vegetables for about 30 minutes, turning occasionally, until tender and cooked through. Drain well, sprinkle with chopped parsley and serve with a green salad and some crusty bread.

COOK'S TIP
Maple syrup adds a subtle sweetness, but it is quite expensive. For a more economical version, use 2 tablespoons light brown sugar.

Preparation time	10 minutes
Cooking time	2 hours, plus 30 minutes resting
Calories per portion	440 Kcal
Fat per portion	23.5g
of which saturated	9.8g
Serves	6

Spiced roast gammon

A smoked gammon joint stuffed with delicious fruit and spice.

Butter 25g (1oz), softened
Cox's apple 1 large, peeled, cored and chopped
Pitted prunes 110g (4oz), chopped
Ground cinnamon 1 tsp
Freshly ground black pepper
Smoked gammon joint 1.6kg (3½lb), outer rind removed in one piece and reserved
Clear honey 2 tbsp
Demerara sugar 2–3 tbsp
Lemon 1, juice only

Preheat the oven to 180°C/350°F/Gas 4. In a bowl, blend the butter with the apple, prunes and cinnamon, and season with pepper. With a long knife, make a cut through the centre of the gammon, then fill it with the stuffing and secure with skewers.

Place the gammon on a rack in a roasting tin, cover with the gammon rind and foil and cook for 1¼ hours. Remove from the oven, take off the foil and rind and then spread with the honey and sugar.

Add the lemon juice and 4 tablespoons water to the roasting tin, return to the oven and cook for 30–40 minutes, basting frequently, until the gammon has a golden glaze and is cooked through. If necessary, add more water to the tin to prevent over-browning. Allow the gammon to rest for 30 minutes before carving and then serve a Fruit and nuts salad (see page 7).

COOK'S TIP
If you don't have any demerara sugar, then use soft light or dark muscovado sugar instead.

143

Preparation time	**5 minutes**
Cooking time	**25 minutes**
Calories per portion	**487 Kcal**
Fat per portion	**35g**
of which saturated	**14.7g**
Serves	**4**

Lamb with salad

Tender roast lamb that contrasts beautifully with crisp Greek salad.

Aubergine 1, thinly sliced
Olive oil 4 tbsp
Salt and freshly ground black pepper
Lamb leg, from fillet end 600g (1lb 5oz)
Rosemary 2 sprigs
Cos lettuce 1 heart, washed
Rocket leaves a handful
Feta cheese 200g packet, cubed
Tomatoes 2, cut into large chunks
Cucumber ½, cut into small cubes
Lemon 1

Preheat the oven to 200°C/400°F/ Gas 6. Toss the aubergine in 2 tablespoons of the olive oil and season. Rub a generous amount of salt into the fat of the lamb. Place the lamb in a roasting tin and lay the rosemary on top. Put in the oven to roast. After 15 minutes, spread the aubergine around the meat.

Return to the oven and roast for a further 10 minutes until the meat is cooked but rosy and the vegetables are tender. Remove the roasting tin from the oven and leave it to rest for 5 minutes, keeping it warm.

Place the lettuce, broken into large pieces, on a platter along with the rocket, feta, tomatoes and cucumber. Pour over the remaining olive oil and a squeeze of lemon juice. Season and toss lightly. Top with the cooked aubergine slices.

Carve the lamb into thick slices and lay over the salad. Serve immediately with some good crusty bread.

COOK'S TIP
Other Mediterranean vegetables can be used in this recipe. Roast rounds of courgettes or thin slices of red pepper in the same way as the aubergine.

Preparation time	15 minutes
Cooking time	1 hour 50 minutes
Calories per portion	868 Kcal
Fat per portion	44g
of which saturated	19.2g
Serves	4

Mediterranean-style roast lamb

Gorgeous garlicky lamb roasted to perfection with vegetables and tomato sauce.

Whole leg lamb 1.65–1.8kg (3½–4lb)
Garlic 2 cloves, peeled and crushed
Wholegrain or Dijon mustard 2 tbsp
Dried oregano
Salt
Baby new potatoes 500g packet
Leeks 4, trimmed and cut into chunks
Carrots 4, trimmed and quartered
Tomato and basil pasta sauce
500g jar
Sprigs of oregano

Preheat the oven to 180ºC/350ºF/Gas 4. Weigh the lamb to calculate the cooking time. Allow 25 minutes per 450g (1lb) plus 25 minutes. Set the lamb in a roasting tin.

Mix the garlic, mustard, dried oregano and a little salt in a small bowl to make a paste. Brush the paste liberally over the lamb and roast in the oven for about 40 minutes. During this time the fat will begin to run from the joint.

Remove the lamb from the oven (about an hour before the end of cooking time) and quickly add the new potatoes, leeks and carrots. Stir the vegetables in the lamb fat and juices and pop back in the oven for a further 30 minutes.

Remove the lamb from the oven once again. Add the pasta sauce and stir well so that all the vegetables are covered in the sauce (you may need to add a splash of water) and continue cooking for the remaining time. This should be a further 30–40 minutes. The exact time will depend on the size of the lamb joint. Stir the vegetables once during the cooking time.

Carve the lamb and serve with the vegetables and tomato sauce, garnished with sprigs of oregano.

COOK'S TIP
You only need about 3–4 tablespoons of lamb fat to cook the vegetables; if there is more, drain off the excess.

Preparation time	30 minutes
Cooking time	1½–2 hours
Calories per portion	508 Kcal
Fat per portion	26g
of which saturated	10.3g
Serves	4

Baked marrow with mince

Whole marrow filled with tender vegetables and mince with a cheese topping.

Olive oil 2 tbsp
Onion 1 large, peeled and chopped
Carrots 3 large, peeled and cut into small dice
Marrow 1 large
Extra lean minced beef or lamb 500g (1lb 2oz)
Plain flour 25g (1oz)
Tomatoes 3 large, peeled, deseeded and cut into small dice
Tomato purée 2 tbsp
Peas 110g (4oz)
Runner beans 150g (5oz), thinly sliced
Beef or chicken stock 150ml (¼ pint)
Worcestershire sauce 1 tbsp
Mixed dried herbs 2 tbsp
Goats' cheese 110g (4oz), sliced
Paprika

Preheat the oven to 200°C/400°F/Gas 6.

Heat the oil in a flameproof roasting tin, add the onion and carrots and cook gently together for 10 minutes, taking care not to let them brown. Meanwhile, cut a slice lengthways off the top of the marrow, approximately a quarter of the way down. Scoop out and discard the seeds and stringy fibres from the top and the bottom. Cut a thin sliver from the bottom of the marrow – to stop it rolling.

Add the beef to the roasting tin and cook, stirring, until the meat changes colour. Then stir in the flour, tomatoes, tomato purée, peas and beans, stock, Worcestershire sauce and herbs.

Fill the marrow with the beef mixture and place in the roasting tin. Cover the filling with the top slice of marrow, and add 2–3 tablespoons of water to the tin.

Cover the marrow closely with a sheet of foil, then cook in the centre of the oven for approximately 1½–2 hours until the marrow is cooked (time will vary according to the thickness of the marrow's flesh).

Remove the marrow from the oven and take off the foil. Scatter over the goats' cheese and return to the oven for 10 minutes, or until the cheese is browned. Sprinkle with paprika and serve.

COOK'S TIP
Alternatively, cut the marrow into 5cm (2in) thick slices, hollow out the centre and fill with the beans, peas and beef mixture. Cook as in the method.

Preparation time	**20 minutes**
Cooking time	**1 hour**
Calories per portion	**539 Kcal**
Fat per portion	**33g**
of which saturated	**15.8g**
Serves	**4**

Roast pheasant

Rich, gamey pheasant roasted with bacon and mushrooms.

Fresh pheasant 1 brace, rinsed with cold water then dried with kitchen towel
Butter 50g (2oz)
Salt and freshly ground black pepper
Thyme small bunch
Smoked streaky bacon 8 rashers
Watercress to garnish
Cup mushrooms 110g (4oz), sliced
Plain flour 2 tbsp
Brandy 2 tbsp
Chicken stock 300ml (½ pint)
Madeira or Marsala wine 3 tbsp
Double cream 3 tbsp

COOK'S TIP
It is important that the brandy is bubbling before you set fire to it. If the alcohol content isn't heated sufficiently, it won't set alight.

Preheat the oven to 190°C/375°F/Gas 5. Put the pheasants in a roasting tin, spread the butter over the breasts and legs, season lightly and top each bird with a few sprigs of thyme. Lay the bacon rashers on top and loosely cover with foil.

Roast for 45 minutes. Remove the foil, lift the bacon off the pheasant breasts and leave in the tin. Spoon the meat juices over and roast for 15 minutes more until browned and the meat juices run clear when the larger pheasant is tested with a skewer through the leg into the breast.

Garnish with watercress then transfer to a serving plate. Add the mushrooms to the meat juices in the roasting tin and fry for 3 minutes until golden.

Stir in the flour then add the brandy. When bubbling, flame with a match and stand well back. After the flames have subsided, stir in the stock and wine and bring to the boil, stirring until smooth. Mix in the cream and season to taste.

Pour the sauce into a sauceboat. Carve the pheasant or cut into joints with poultry shears. Spoon around the sauce and serve with a Bean salad (see page 7).

Preparation time	10 minutes
Cooking time	40 minutes, plus
	10 minutes standing
Calories per portion	203 Kcal
Fat per portion	10g
of which saturated	6.5g
Serves	4

Suitable for vegetarians

Slow-roast pears with orange & aniseed

Roast pears with the fragrant sweet taste of star anise.

Ripe pears 4
Lemon 1, juice only
Oranges 2 large
Light brown sugar 2 tbsp
Star anise 3
Unsalted butter 50g (2oz)
Double cream or natural yogurt

Preheat the oven to 180°C/350°F/Gas 4.

Peel, core and halve the pears. Place in a small, shallow roasting tin and toss in the lemon juice.

Using a sharp knife, slice the top and bottom off the oranges, and slice off the rind, taking away as much of the white pith as possible. Cut each orange into 4 thick slices, remove any seeds and carefully mix into the pears.

Sprinkle over the sugar, add the star anise and dot with butter. Bake for 20 minutes, basting occasionally, then carefully turn over and continue to cook for a further 20 minutes, continuing to baste occasionally. Allow to stand for 10 minutes before serving and discard the star anise.

The pears are best served warm with the juices spooned over and accompanied by double cream or natural yogurt.

COOK'S TIP
By allowing the pears to stand for a few minutes before serving, they cool slightly and the flavours of the dish develop further.

Bowl

You'll be bowled over by the different ways of cooking and preparing food in a bowl! One lovely thing about these recipes (apart from their tastiness) is that the bowl makes an attractive serving dish, too.

Two dishes that mostly just need to be chilled are the classic chilled soup Gazpacho and the wonderfully exotic Savoury summer pudding. Cooked dishes such as Warm tuna pasta and Quick fishy rice just require a few minutes in the microwave. Great for a light lunch or to offer other dishes a real lift are the selection of salads, including recipes featuring Raspberry, mango & Stilton, Avocado & grapefruit and the Fruity Greek and Layered coronation chicken options. To finish is a choice of desserts offering freshness and flavour, such as Mango granita or Fresh fruit compote or, for a touch of indulgence, a refreshing Pink grapefruit syllabub or a classic coffee and rum Tiramisu.

Preparation time **45 minutes, plus 3–4 hours chilling**

Calories per portion **115 Kcal**

Fat per portion **7.9g**

of which saturated **1.1g**

Serves **6**

Suitable for vegetarians

Gazpacho

Chilled Spanish tomato and vegetable soup scattered with croûtons.

Cucumber 225g (8oz)
Plum tomatoes 4 large
Onion 1 small, peeled
Green pepper 1 small, cored and deseeded
Red pepper 1 small, deseeded
Garlic 2–3 cloves, peeled
Fresh white breadcrumbs 25g (1oz)
Vegetable stock 750ml (1¼ pints)
Red wine vinegar 2 tbsp
Olive oil 4 tbsp
Salt and freshly ground black pepper
Croûtons
Basil leaves

Roughly chop the cucumber, tomatoes, onion, peppers and garlic and place in a large bowl. Add the breadcrumbs, stock, vinegar and olive oil. Mix well, cover and leave to stand for 30 minutes.

Blend the vegetables, in batches, in a food processor or blender to make a coarse textured soup. Season well, cover and chill for 3–4 hours.

Serve the gazpacho topped with croûtons and basil leaves.

COOK'S TIP
For a bloody Mary-style version of this soup, pep up with a dash of Tabasco and Worcestershire sauce.

Preparation time	15 minutes, plus overnight chilling
Calories per portion	354 Kcal
Fat per portion	13g
of which saturated	1.8g
Serves	6

Suitable for vegetarians

Savoury summer pudding

The naturally sweet taste of artichokes and tomatoes with focaccia.

Focaccia bread 2 rectangular loaves approximately 15 x 11cm (6 x 4in)
Passata with herbs 500g carton
Tomatoes 3, chopped
Black pitted olives 50g (2oz), chopped
Sun-dried tomatoes 50g (2oz), chopped
Antipasto artichokes 285g jar, drained
Spring onions 3, trimmed and chopped
Salt and freshly ground black pepper
Basil leaves

Cut the focaccia into 1cm (½in) slices. Cut two slices to fit the base of a 1.5 litre (2½ pint) basin and arrange more round the sides, overlapping them slightly. Reserve four slices for the top.

Mix all the other ingredients together in a large bowl and season well. Spoon the tomato mixture into the bread-lined basin, packing it in as you go. Cover with the remaining bread slices. Seal tightly with cling film and top with a plate and a weight. Transfer to the fridge and leave overnight.

When you are ready to serve, turn out the pudding onto a plate and top with some basil leaves. Serve with a Dressed leaves salad (see page 7).

COOK'S TIP
Don't be tempted to turn this dish out of the basin after just a few hours or you will find it will collapse.

Preparation time **10 minutes**
Calories per portion **279 Kcal**
Fat per portion **21g**
of which saturated **7.8g**
Serves **4**
Suitable for vegetarians

Raspberry, mango & Stilton salad

A tangy yet fruity salad with the distinctive taste of Stilton.

Raspberry vinegar 6 tbsp
Olive oil 4 tbsp
Dijon mustard 1 tsp
Caster sugar 1 tsp
Salt and freshly ground black pepper
Raspberries 250g (9oz)
Mango 1 peeled, stoned and cubed
Stilton cheese 110g (4oz), cubed
Salad leaves 150g bag

To make the dressing, pour the raspberry vinegar and olive oil into a bowl and add the mustard, sugar and seasoning. Whisk the dressing to mix together the ingredients. Add half the raspberries to the bowl and use a fork to mash them slightly into the dressing. Stir the mango and cheese into the dressing.

Divide the salad leaves between four plates. Spoon over the mango and cheese and scatter over the remaining raspberries, drizzling over any remaining dressing Serve immediately with some crusty bread to mop up the dressing.

COOK'S TIP
If possible, choose a bag of salad that contains some shredded beetroot as the deep red colour looks good with the red raspberries and orange mango.

Preparation time	**15 minutes**
Calories per portion	**198 Kcal**
Fat per portion	**12g**
of which saturated	**6.6g**
Serves	**4**
Suitable for vegetarians	

Fruity Greek salad

A minty combination with crisp salad, watermelon and crumbly feta.

Cos lettuce ½
Vine tomatoes 6, diced
Red onion 1 small, peeled and sliced into rings
Green pepper 1, deseeded and chopped
Cucumber ¼, halved, deseeded and sliced
Pitted back olives 50g (2oz)
Watermelon 1 thick slice
Feta cheese 200g (7oz), lightly crumbled
Ready-made mint sauce 1 tbsp
Cider or white wine vinegar 2 tbsp
Clear honey 1 tsp
Freshly ground black pepper

Discard any damaged outer leaves from the lettuce. Break up the leaves, rinse and shake them dry. Rip the leaves into bite-sized pieces and put in a serving bowl.

Toss the tomatoes, onion, pepper, cucumber and olives into the leaves and set aside.

Remove the skin and seeds from the watermelon and cut into bite-sized pieces. Toss into the salad along with the feta cheese.

Mix the mint sauce with the vinegar and honey and drizzle over the salad. Season with black pepper and serve.

COOK'S TIP
Watermelons are usually large, but are often available in halves or slices. Alternatively, look out for ready prepared slices or pieces in pre-packed fruit salad mixes.

Preparation time	20 minutes
Calories per portion	244 Kcal
Fat per portion	22g
of which saturated	2.8g
Serves	4

Suitable for vegetarians

Avocado & grapefruit salad

Rich avocado and grapefruit warmed with a chilli dressing.

Pink or red blush grapefruit 1
Olive oil 3 tbsp
Clear honey 1 tsp
Red chilli ½–1, depending on heat, deseeded and finely sliced
Spring onions 2–3, trimmed and finely sliced
Firm tofu 110g (4oz), cut into small cubes
Avocados 2
Mint leaves good handful
Salt and freshly ground black pepper
Romaine or cos lettuce 1, leaves separated and shredded
Country style bread

COOK'S TIP
Tofu is fairly bland so if you have time, leave it marinating in the dressing for 20 minutes or so before adding the avocado.

Cut the ends off the top and bottom of the unpeeled grapefruit, then cut off the peel and pith. Hold the fruit over a large bowl to catch the juice while cutting in between the segments. There should be 2–3 tablespoons of juice. Keep the segments on the chopping board.

To make the dressing, whisk the oil, honey, chilli and spring onions into the juice in the bowl. Add the tofu cubes, then peel, halve, stone and dice the avocado and toss the pieces, with the grapefruit segments, into the dressing with a few mint leaves, finely sliced. Season lightly.

Add a few more mint leaves as a garnish just before serving portions on to beds of the shredded romaine or cos lettuce. Serve with chunks of bread.

Preparation time	5 minutes
Cooking time	7 minutes
Calories per portion	633 Kcal
Fat per portion	37g
of which saturated	5.3g
Serves	2

Warm tuna pasta

Salade niçoise, warmed and combined with penne pasta.

Fresh penne 150g (5oz)
Green beans 50g (2oz), stalks trimmed, cut into short lengths
Boiling water 450ml (¾ pint)
Marinated and grilled artichoke hearts 4 halved hearts (see Cook's tip)
Baby plum tomatoes 8, halved

Anchovies 50g can, drained, anchovies roughly chopped
Tuna fish in olive oil 185g can
Black olives 6
Red wine vinegar 1 tbsp
Freshly ground black pepper
Basil leaves handful, finely chopped
Parsley leaves handful, finely chopped

Put the pasta and cut beans into a large microwave-proof serving bowl. Pour in the boiling water and cover with a lid (or film and pierce it). Open the steam holes and cook on 'high' for 5 minutes. Drain off the water.

Quarter the artichoke hearts and add them to the bowl together with the tomato halves and anchovies and 3 tablespoons of oil from the can of tuna. Cover again and cook on 'high' for a further minute.

Break the tuna into large chunks and add to the pasta with the olives, red wine vinegar and black pepper. Cook on 'high' for 1 minute until just warmed through.

Mix the basil and parsley leaves into the salad and serve immediately.

COOK'S TIP
If you can't find artichoke hearts in the deli section, look for the jars of them. Other jars or tubs from the deli section are always handy to keep in store for adding to pasta.

Preparation time	**10 minutes**
Cooking time	**20 minutes**
Calories per portion	**464 Kcal**
Fat per portion	**7g**
of which saturated	**1.5g**
Serves	**4**

Quick fishy rice

A zesty, tasty mixture of rice, bacon and cod.

Leek 1, trimmed and thinly sliced
Smoked back bacon 4 rashers, cut
into finger-width strips
Hot fish or vegetable stock 500ml
(18fl oz)
Easy-cook long grain rice 300g
(11oz)
Smoked cod or haddock 500g
(1lb 2oz), skinned and cut into large
chunks
Frozen peas 100g (3½oz)
Capers 1 tbsp (optional)
Chopped parsley 3 tbsp
Lemon ½, grated zest and juice
**Salt and freshly ground black
pepper**

Put the leek in a large microwave-
proof bowl and lay the bacon strips on
top. Add 4 tablespoons of the stock.
Cover with a lid (or film and pierce it)
and microwave on 'high' for 5 minutes
(all microwave instructions are for
'high' in this recipe).

Stir in the rice together with the rest
of the stock and cook, uncovered, for
7 minutes.

Gently stir in the fish chunks, cover
with the lid or film and cook for 5
minutes. Then add the peas and cook
for another 3 minutes until the fish and
rice are cooked.

Stir in the capers, if using, and the
parsley, lemon zest and juice, only a
little salt (as the fish will be salty), and
lots of black pepper. Leave to stand
for a couple of minutes and then
serve from the bowl, accompanied by
Dressed leaves (see page 7).

COOK'S TIP
Keep the fish in biggish chunks otherwise it
tends to fall apart with cooking and stirring.

Preparation time	15 minutes, plus
	1 hour chilling
Calories per portion	519 Kcal
Fat per portion	21g
of which saturated	5.4g
Serves	2

Layered coronation chicken salad

Gently spiced chicken with juicy mango, pepper and tomato.

Cooked skinless chicken 350g
(12oz), cut into bite-sized pieces
Low fat natural fromage frais 3 tbsp
Reduced calorie mayonnaise 3 tbsp
Mild curry powder 1½ tsp
Mango 1
Mixed small salad leaves 115g bag
Yellow pepper 1, deseeded and
sliced into thin rings
Vine tomatoes 2 large, thinly sliced
Cayenne pepper

In a bowl, mix together the chicken pieces with the fromage frais, mayonnaise and curry powder.

Peel the skin from the mango, then slice down either side of the smooth flat central stone and cut the flesh into thin slices.

In individual glass bowls, layer the ingredients as follows: mango slices, salad leaves, yellow pepper, tomato, more salad leaves and then the chicken mix. Top with a sprinkling of cayenne pepper.

COOK'S TIP
For a tasty alternative, try using large peeled prawns instead of the chicken, or replace the mango with a sliced fresh peach or nectarine.

Preparation time	20 minutes, plus chilli
Calories per portion	**74 Kcal**
Fat per portion	**0.3g**
of which saturated	**0g**
Serves	**4**

Suitable for vegetarians

Green tea fruit salad

Fragrant fruit with a dash of sherry.

Japanese green tea bag 1
Kiwi fruit 2
Lychees 225g (8oz)
Green-fleshed melon such as Galia ¼
Seedless green grapes 110g (4oz)
Dry sherry 2 tbsp (optional)
Lime 1, grated zest and juice
Caster sugar

Place the tea bag in a small heatproof jug and pour over 150ml (¼ pint) boiling water. Leave to infuse for 5 minutes, then discard the bag and allow the tea to cool. Cover and chill for 30 minutes.

Peel and thinly slice the kiwi fruit and peel, halve and stone the lychees. Remove the seeds from the melon and slice off the skin. Cut the flesh into small pieces. Separate the grapes from their stalks. Put all the fruits into a bowl, cover and chill until required.

Once the tea has cooled, mix in the sherry, if using, lime zest (reserving some to decorate) and juice and add sufficient sugar to taste.

To serve, arrange the fruits in four serving bowls and drizzle over the tea mixture. Decorate with the reserved lime rind and serve.

COOK'S TIP
If fresh lychees are unavailable, look out for them in cans. You will need to drain them well and rinse off the syrup. Otherwise, replace the lychees with chunks of fresh pineapple.

Preparation time	5 minutes, plus
	3 hours freezing
Calories per portion	130 Kcal
Fat per portion	0.5g
of which saturated	0.1g
Serves	8
Suitable for vegetarians	

Mango granita

Refreshing frozen dessert with mango and raspberries.

Mangoes 2 large, peeled and stoned
Mango and passion fruit smoothie
1 litre carton

COOK'S TIP
Traditionally, granita is made from sugar
syrup and flavouring. This is a healthy, quick
and easy version packed full of fruit. It is the
perfect dessert to serve after a spicy meal.

Tip the mango flesh into a food processor and whizz until smooth. With the
motor still running, gradually pour in the mango and passion fruit smoothie.

Pour the mango purée into a rigid plastic container, cover and freeze for about 3
hours. Then remove from the freezer, stir well and freeze until firm.

The texture of your final granita is up to you. For a smooth sorbet style granita,
keep mixing every few hours to break down the ice crystals and re-freeze.

If you like large, coarse ice crystals, after stirring once, leave in the freezer until
firm. Then, using the prongs of a fork, scrape the granita into individual glasses
and serve immediately.

163

Preparation time	5 minutes
Cooking time	3 minutes
Calories per portion	134 Kcal
Fat per portion	0g
of which saturated	0.1g
Serves	3
Suitable for vegetarians	

Fresh fruit compote

Sweet and gently warmed fruit with yogurt.

Pink grapefruit 1 large, peeled
Orange juice 4 tbsp
Honey 1 generous tbsp, plus extra to drizzle
Ground ginger ½ tsp
Dried berries and cherries 4 tbsp
Pear 1 large, unpeeled or peeled, cut into 8 wedges and cored
Banana 1 large, peeled and cut into 8 chunky slices
Yogurt

Segment the grapefruit into a medium-sized bowl. Add the orange juice, honey, ginger and dried fruits and then add the pear and banana.

Microwave on 'medium' for 2 minutes, stir, then microwave for another minute until warmed. Serve warm with a dollop of yogurt on each bowl topped with a drizzle of honey.

COOK'S TIP
It's fine to use fresh orange juice from a carton if you haven't any oranges to squeeze.

Preparation time	30 minutes, plus
	3–4 hours chilling
Calories per portion	417 Kcal
Fat per portion	40.3g
of which saturated	22.6g
Serves	4
Suitable for vegetarians	

Pink grapefruit syllabub

A light and fluffy combination of cream, wine and grapefruit.

Pink grapefruit 1 large
Lemon juice 2 tbsp
Medium dry white wine 60ml (2fl oz)
Caster sugar 25g (1oz)
Double cream 300ml (½ pint)

Using a lemon zester or grater, remove the zest from the grapefruit and put it into a bowl, taking care not to remove any of the white pith as this will make the syllabub bitter.

Cut the grapefruit in half, squeeze out the juice from one half only and add it to the bowl (use some of the remaining half of the grapefruit for decoration – see below – squeeze the rest for drinking). Add the lemon juice, white wine and caster sugar and stir until the sugar is dissolved. Then cover and refrigerate to 1–2 hours.

Add the cream and use a hand whisk or hand-held electric mixer to whisk the mixture slowly until it becomes light and fluffy and holds a trail when drizzled across the surface.

Carefully spoon the syllabub into chilled wine or sundae glasses. Cover with cling film and refrigerate for 3–4 hours. Just before serving, decorate the syllabubs with small triangles of chopped grapefruit and serve with a biscuit.

COOK'S TIP
At first, do not use the whisk on full speed as the mixture will splatter. Use medium to low, and then increase the speed as the mixture thickens.

Preparation time	**15 minutes, plus**
	1 hour chilling
Calories per portion	**572 Kcal**
Fat per portion	**37g**
of which saturated	**20.6g**
Serves	**4**
Suitable for vegetarians	

Tiramisu

Coffee and rum biscuits, topped with mascarpone.

Sponge fingers 75g (6oz)
Strong espresso coffee 125ml (4fl oz)
Coffee liqueur, such as Kahlua or rum 4 tbsp
Eggs 3, yolks only
Caster sugar 75g (3oz)
Mascarpone 250g pot
Cocoa powder for decorating

Break half the sponge fingers into small enough pieces to fit into the bottom of four tumbler glasses. In a measuring jug, mix together the coffee and liqueur and pour half over the biscuits.

In a bowl, whisk together the egg yolks and sugar until light, thick and fluffy. Then gradually whisk in the mascarpone.

Spoon half the mascarpone mixture on top of the coffee and liqueur and sift over a layer of cocoa powder. Then add the remaining sponge fingers and coffee and liqueur, followed by the rest of the mascarpone.

Chill for at least an hour so that the flavours have time to develop. Before serving, lightly sift cocoa powder over the top to decorate.

COOK'S TIP
For a richer version, swap the cocoa powder for grated chocolate.

Preparation time	**30 minutes, plus chilling time**
Calories per portion	**479 Kcal**
Fat per portion	**41g**
of which saturated	**22.7g**
Serves	**6**
Suitable for vegetarians	

Orange cream

Tangy, yet sweet and creamy – a delectable combination.

Trifle sponges 6, cut in half lengthways
Oranges 3 large, grated rind and juice of 2, plus segments of 1
Lemon 1, grated rind and juice
Sugar 25g (1oz)
Double cream 450ml (¾ pint)
Orange and lemon rind curls to decorate, optional

Place the sponge slices in a large serving bowl so that they cover the base and come halfway up the sides. Cover with the orange segments.

Mix the citrus rind and juice with the sugar in a bowl, until it is completely dissolved. Add the cream and whisk together until it is light and thickened.

Pour the mixture over the sponge and refrigerate overnight. Decorate with orange and lemon rind curls (if using) and serve.

COOK'S TIP
Take care not to over-whip the cream and juice mixture as it could separate.

Preparation time	**1 hour 15 minutes**
Calories per portion	**447 Kcal**
Fat per portion	**30.2g**
of which saturated	**18.8g**
Serves	**4**

Suitable for freezing

Rhubarb & ginger fool

Custard and cream whipped with rhubarb and fiery ginger.

Cold cooked rhubarb 900ml
(1½ pints)
Cold thick custard 225ml (8fl oz)
Double cream 225ml (8fl oz)
Ginger syrup 4 tbsp (from stem
ginger) (optional)
Stem ginger 1 tbsp, chopped
(optional)
**Thin ginger biscuits or shortbread
biscuits**

COOK'S TIP
For the best flavour, use garden rhubarb.
If wished, a little pink colouring may be
added to the fool mixture.

Drain the excess juice from the rhubarb and place in a large serving bowl. Pour
in the cold custard and fold into the rhubarb.

In a medium-sized bowl, whisk the cream until it holds a soft, floppy peak (with
ginger syrup, if using). Then gently fold into the rhubarb, cover and chill well – for
at least 1 hour.

To serve, sprinkle with chopped ginger (if using), and accompany with ginger
biscuits or shortbread.

169

Preparation time	**10 minutes**
Cooking time	**6 minutes**
Calories per portion	**354 Kcal**
Fat per portion	**18g**
of which saturated	**10.2g**
Serves	**6**

Suitable for vegetarians

Speedy orange syrup pudding

Fluffy sponge pudding, topped with orange and syrup.

Golden syrup 2 tbsp, plus extra for serving (optional)
Orange 1
Butter 110g (4oz), softened
Caster sugar 110g (4oz)
Eggs 2
Self-raising flour 175g (6oz)
Custard or double cream

Generously butter a 1.25 litre (2 pint) pudding basin and then spoon in the golden syrup. Use a zester or grater to take the rind off the orange into a larger mixing bowl. Remove the rind then segment the orange, catching the juices in the mixing bowl (there should be about 2 tablespoons). Arrange the orange segments in the syrup in the pudding basin.

Add the butter and sugar to the orange zest and juice in the mixing bowl and beat until light and fluffy.

Beat in the eggs with a little of the flour then fold in the rest of flour with a tablespoon of warm water, to make the mixture a smooth dropping consistency.

Spoon the pudding mixture over the oranges in the syrup, cover with cling film and microwave on 'high' for 6 minutes in an 800-watt microwave oven. Adjust the time for a cooker of a different wattage.

Leave to stand for a minute or two, then turn out onto a warmed serving plate. The orange segments will have broken up to make a soft sauce on top of the pudding. Spoon over more syrup, warmed, if you like, then serve straightaway with custard or cream.

COOK'S TIP
Check the pudding with a skewer after 5 minutes, then add another minute if necessary. But take care, as overcooking makes the sponge hard and dry.

Index

Previous books

Dairy Cookbooks are recognised as some of the most reliable recipe books ever written. With over 30 million copies sold, most households will have used a Dairy Cookbook at some point.

The first book – The Dairy Book of Home Cookery – was published in 1968 and has been revised and reprinted several times due to its unprecedented popularity.

The Dairy Book of Home Cookery

(416 pages) was last published in 1992, and contains hundreds of recipes, from how to make the perfect cheese sauce to creating an impressive soufflé.
Now in its third reprint!

In recent years, six new best-selling cookbooks have been published:

The New Dairy Cookbook

(192 pages) was published in 2001 and features 150 delicious new recipes for all occasions.

Quick & Easy Dairy Cookbook

(192 pages) was published in 2003 and has 130 tasty recipes, which can be prepared in less than 30 minutes.

Year Round Dairy Cookbook

(192 pages), published in 2005 and features 130 seasonal recipes to give the taste buds a treat the whole year round.

Around Britain Dairy Cookbook

(192 pages) was published in 2006 and contains favourite regional recipes plus new ones with a contemporary twist.

Hearty & Healthy

(192 pages) was published in 2007 and contains recipes to help you eat well, keep well and enjoy good food.

Clever Cooking for One or Two

(192 pages) was published in 2008 and contains mouthwatering recipes for one or two that are simple to prepare with no waste.

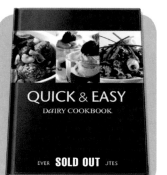

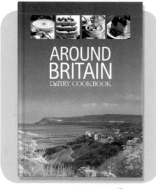

For more information and availability visit the Dairy Diary website at www.dairydiary.co.uk